CHAMPION OF FREEDOM
AUNG SAN SUU KYI

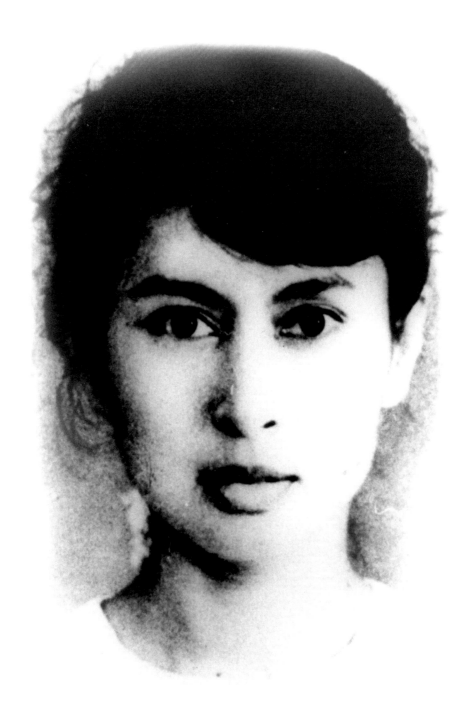

CHAMPION OF FREEDOM
AUNG SAN SUU KYI

SHERRY O'KEEFE

GREENSBORO, NORTH CAROLINA

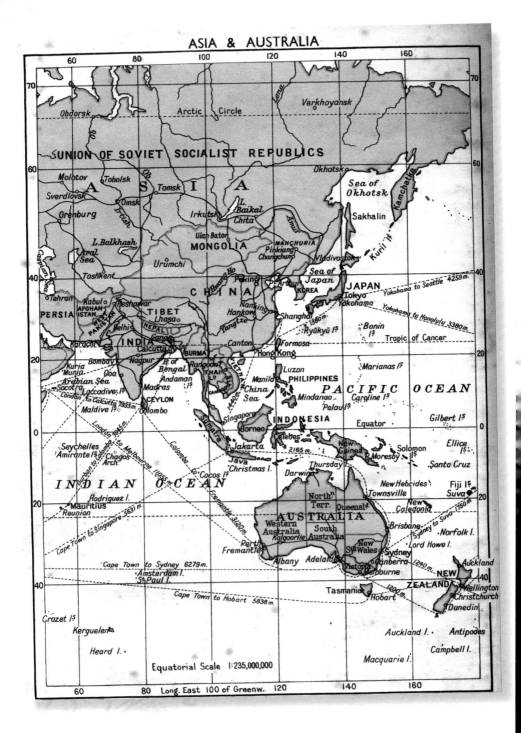

Burma is located southeast of India.

To Will and Beth's grand and great grandparents
for the hard lives they lived in order to choose freedom,
and to their future grand and great grandchildren
for the hard choices they will one day also make

A view of Rangoon, Burma

CHAMPION OF FREEDOM
AUNG SAN SUU KYI
Copyright © 2012 by Morgan Reynolds Publishing

For more information write:
Morgan Reynolds Publishing, Inc.
620 South Elm Street, Suite 387
Greensboro, NC 27406 USA

Library of Congress Cataloging-in-Publication Data

O'Keefe, Sherry.
Champion of freedom : Aung San Suu Kyi / by Sherry O'Keefe. -- 1st ed.
   p. cm.
Includes bibliographical references and index.
ISBN 978-1-59935-168-1 -- ISBN 978-1-59935-314-2 (e-book) 1. Aung
San
Suu Kyi--Juvenile literature. 2. Women political
activists--Burma--Biography--Juvenile literature. 3. Women political
prisoners--Burma--Biography--Juvenile literature. 4. Women Nobel Prize
winners--Burma--Biographpy--Juvenile literature. 5.
Democracy--Burma--Juvenile literature. 6. Burma--Politics and
government--1988---Juvenile literature. I. Title.
DS530.53.A85O44 2012
959.105092--dc23
[B]
                              2011035740

PRINTED IN THE UNITED STATES OF AMERICA
First Edition

Book cover and interior designed by:
Ed Morgan, navyblue design studio
Greensboro, NC

TABLE OF CONTENTS

Aung San Suu Kyi as a girl

BURMA:
"LAND OF CHARM AND CRUELTY"

Aung San Suu Kyi was "terribly frightened of the dark" as a child growing up in Rangoon, a city in the Southeast Asian country of Burma. "I think I was afraid of ghosts," she said, "because the Burmese are very fond of ghost stories."

At age twelve, Suu Kyi decided to conquer her fear. In the evening, her mother would make hot milk for Suu Kyi and her brothers. But Suu Kyi liked her milk cold, so she'd let it sit in a downstairs room until it had cooled. Later, in the dark, she'd leave her upstairs room and go downstairs to drink her milk. "The first few days my heart would go 'thump, thump, thump,' but after five or six days I got quite used to it.

"I wandered around in the darkness until I knew where all the demons might be . . . they weren't there."

That early experience of finding a way to conquer fear would serve Suu Kyi well in later years. As an adult, she would follow in her famous father's footsteps and dedicate her life to fighting for democracy and human rights in Burma—and, as a result, suffer decades of detention by the repressive, military-backed Burmese government and even the threat of death.

Through it all, Suu Kyi has never let fear dissuade her from fighting for what she believes is right. "The only real prison is fear," she believes, "and the only real freedom is freedom from fear."

Aung San Suu Kyi was born on June 19, 1945, in Rangoon. She was the third and last child born to her mother Khin Kyi and her father, General Aung San. Aung San had just commanded Burma's revolutionary army to victory over the Japanese and was well on his way to leading his country to freedom and independence.

That war for independence from Japan was part of Burma's longstanding struggle against foreign occupation that dated back to 1824, when British invaders first crossed into Burma on a mission to colonize. After waging war for more than a half-century, in 1885 Great Britain finally emerged victorious. It annexed Burma as a province of its greater Indian empire and set up a colonial government in Rangoon that would rule until the outbreak of World War II—just before Suu Kyi was born.

Under British rule, Rangoon developed into a bustling, "vividly cosmopolitan [city that] outshone Bangkok and rivaled Singapore." At its center lay the ancient Shwedagon Pagoda, the grand Buddhist temple built after the Buddha's death in the fifth century BCE. After the imperial takeover, Burma became primed

The British arrive in Mandalay, Burma, in 1885.

An 1825 lithograph of the Shwedagon Pagoda

for British exploitation. Commercial buildings, cinemas, clubs, stadiums, and trading outlets cropped up around the city, as did churches and other cultural and religious centers. Great Britain profited tremendously from the riches that this growth and expansion produced, but Burma benefited in some ways, too. Its people were not free or self-governed, but with economic development came some prosperity and advancement. The construction of an interregional rail network, for example, helped spread some wealth and—more significantly—ideas throughout the country.

Revolutionary Change

As the colonial age dragged on, the idea of independence began gathering steam in Burma. Wind of such ideas as freedom and democracy had come to Southeast Asia via Europe, and some of the first anti-colonial, national independence movements developed in neighboring India and French Indo-China (modern-day Laos, Vietnam, and Cambodia). Similar revolutionary sentiment welled up in Burma, too, and eventually most of the country rallied behind the movement for national independence.

The movement for independence helped unify Burma's different ethnic groups. Before the British came to conquer, ethnic-based infighting had torn apart Burma for centuries. Its largest ethnic group was the Burmans. Their chief rivals were the Karens, who, along with the Shans, Chins, Kachins, and Karennis, were scattered about the country. The British extended special favor to the Karens, who converted to Christianity and remained loyal to the Commonwealth through World War II, in some cases even fighting on the side of the British against the Burmese national army.

Great Britain used Burma's ethnic divisions to its advantage, exacerbating tensions between different groups so as to keep the nation divided and politically weak. As long as Burmese people could not get along, Great Britain's hegemony was secure. That began to change during the 1930s, when Burma's ethnic groups began setting aside their differences. It was only through the provoking of Burma's leaders during that war, chief among them Suu

Kyi's father Aung San, that the country's ethnic groups set aside their differences and pledged allegiance to a united, independent Burma.

Suu Kyi's ancestors had played leading roles in the three wars against the British, and they would be instrumental in the independence movement, too. U Min Yaung, a cousin of Suu Kyi's great-grandmother, was among the first to take up arms against the British. When King Thibaw, the last ruler of the Myanmar (another name by which Burma is known) monarchy, absconded to India in 1885, he appointed U Min Yaung chief

King Thibaw, the last ruler of the Burmese monarchy, circa 1880

of a township in central Burma. The British eventually captured and decapitated U Min Yaung, making him a martyr and hero. U Min Yaung's patriotism and revolutionary zeal eventually found similar expression in Suu Kyi's father, Aung San, who would rise to become a national hero in the struggle for independence.

Aung San was born in Natmauk, not far from where U Min Yaung sat as chief. He was the youngest of six children, and his mother indulged him somewhat excessively. He had a quiet disposition, likely the product of his mother's pampering, and until he was four his parents believed he might be mute and dumb. Even when Aung San found his voice, his parents were worried by his refusal to leave for school like his older siblings had done. Despite being exceedingly capable, at home he fell behind for his age academically. Eventually he outgrew his quiet, homebody personality, and once at school he progressed rapidly, catching up with the other pupils and graduating early.

After earning his high school degree Aung San enrolled at Rangoon University. Though somewhat awkward socially, he was a handsome man, admired for his determination, integrity, and work ethic. He was also known, if not notorious, for his outspokenness, and the university expelled him briefly in 1936 for publishing an article in the campus newspaper that mocked school authorities. He was not its author, but his role in publishing the article earned him respect from fellow students. He did not actually graduate from university, but his leadership of the newspaper and political activism positioned him to take charge in the emerging national independence movement.

That movement had started gaining momentum while Aung San was still in secondary school. In December 1930, a former monk and schoolteacher named Saya San had launched a violent rebellion against the British that lasted almost two years. A year into the rebellion British forces captured Saya San, and a few months later they finally crushed the movement. Many British shrugged off San's uprising as being a crazed rampage, but one eyewitness, Englishman Maurice Collis, had a feeling of foreboding about it. In his 1937 book *Trials of Burma*, Collis issued something of a warning:

The peasants rose because that was their way of expressing national dislike of a foreign government. Every man and woman in Burma wanted to get rid of the English government, not because it was oppressive or lacking in good qualities, but because its policy was pro-English instead of being pro-Burman.

THE DOBAMA ASIAYONE

By 1939 Aung San had climbed the ranks of leadership in Burma's revolutionary circles to become general secretary of the Dobama Asiayone—literally, "We Burmese Association." The Dobama Asiayone, as well as the "Freedom Bloc" that Aung San founded, existed to unite Burma's peoples and overthrow the British. Initially the Dobama Asiayone ruled out a coup or revolutionary uprising, hoping to bring about change peacefully. This would require cooperation from the Burmese government, a difficult angle since Prime Minister U Pu was loyal to Great Britain. Aung San wrote a manifesto for the Freedom Bloc and approached U Pu for support, but the prime minister shot down his attempt and dismantled the Freedom Bloc. Aung San was stopped in his tracks and put atop the government's watch list, forcing the Dobama Asiayone to go underground and seek outside support for their cause.

Meanwhile Germany had declared war on Poland, sending chills throughout Europe; the continent seemed on the brink of another war. Germany formed an alliance with Italy and Japan, and the Axis Powers, as the three were known, became Britain's archenemies. Japan's partnership with Germany and Italy globalized the war and forced Britain to defend its interests both at home in Europe and abroad—where especially its colonial holdings in Southeast Asia were contested. Japanese troops had already marched down China's coastline and taken control of major port cities. It was only a matter of time before Tokyo's armies would advance farther west to crush Chiang Kai-shek, leader of the Chinese nationalists whose base was not very far from Burma's northern border.

THE BURMA ROAD

Chiang Kai-shek made headquarters in central-western China and received considerable support from Britain and the United States. With Japan in control of China's main ports, however, most British and American arms and aid supplies to Chiang Kai-shek arrived from India, via the Burma Road. This elevated Burma's strategic importance. In order for the Japanese to defeat the Chinese nationalists and expand their empire into the mainland, it was necessary to cut off Chiang Kai-shek's lifeline—the Burma Road. This sparked Japan's interest in Burma, and before long Burma's movement for national independence became swept up in the larger battle for control of Southeast Asia during World War II.

The Burma Road circa 1944

Chiang Kai-shek

Many Burmese, including Aung San and others in the Dobama Asiayone, sensed an opportunity in the war, namely a chance to overthrow their British conquerors. At a secret Dobama Asiayone conference in early 1940, Aung San proposed that the association seek support from Chinese communists. It was decided that one of them should travel to China on a fund-raising mission. Aung San volunteered, on the condition that he could settle matters as he wished.

Disguised as a deckhand, Aung San traveled by ship to Amoy, China, an international settlement controlled by Japan. After two months of trying to gain favor with the Chinese, he had come up with nothing and was broke and hopeless. Then, a Japanese agent contacted him and conveyed Japan's interest in financing and training the Dobama Asiayone. Aung San saw promise in this proposal and accepted the pledge of support. Japan, not China, would fund and help fight for Burma's independence.

Aung San returned to Burma and recruited a group of men for military leadership training. This band of future commanding officers became known as the "Thirty Heroes," and they left home to begin secret training on the island of Hainan, off the southern coast of China. After continuing on to Formosa, Taiwan, they embarked for Thailand, where they were to raise up an army of Burmese soldiers. Thousands of Burmese were already living in exile in Thailand, and it was from there that the Burmese army, led by Aung San, would join the Japanese on a march to overthrow the British and claim freedom.

THE LAND OF THE BURMESE

European explorers in the fifteenth century described Burma as "the golden land," and the British author and poet Rudyard Kipling called it "the pearl of Asia." Kipling also wrote in his 1889 poem "The Ballad of East and West," in which he famously lamented that "East is East and West is West, and never the twain shall meet," that Burma is "quite unlike any land you know about."

Suu Kyi has described her country as a "land of charm and cruelty."

Burma is slightly smaller than the state of Texas and has a population of somewhere between 49 and 54 million, depending on the reporting source. Ethnic minorities make up one-third of the population, and they occupy more than half of the territory.

Geographically, it is the largest country in Southeast Asia— bordered by China to its north, Laos to its east, Thailand to its southeast, Bangladesh to its west, and India on the northwest, with the Andaman Sea to the south and the Bay of Bengal to the southwest.

The country is rich with petroleum, timber, copper, marble, precious stones, and zinc, among other natural resources. Its climate is tropical, with three distinct seasons: hot (March to May), rainy (June to October), and cool (November to February). Flooding and landslides are common during the rainy season, and the country is prone to destructive earthquakes and cyclones. In early May 2008, Burma was struck by Cyclone Nargis, which claimed more than 138,000 lives and left tens of thousands injured and homeless.

In *Let's Visit Burma*, a 1985 book written by Suu Kyi and published for juveniles, she described her native land in this way:

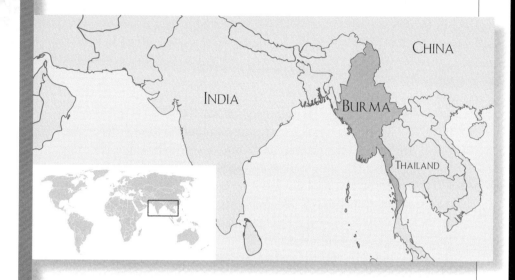

Burma is one of those countries which seem to have been favoured by nature. Its soil is rich, producing rice and other food crops in abundance. There are vast forests containing a large variety of trees from which valuable timber is extracted. Roughly diamond shaped, Burma is often compared to a kite with a tail trailing along one side. The main river is the Irrawaddy which flows from the Kachin Hills in the north and follows a southerly course for . . . (more than one thousand miles) until it reaches the ocean. The capital of Burma is Rangoon, a port city on the delta. "Rangoon" is an English corruption of the Burmese name Yangon, which means "End of Dangers." Rangoon gained importance as a port town in the eighteenth and nineteenth centuries; and, after Burma fell to the British in 1885, it became the capital of the country. . . . The last capital of the Burmese kings was at Mandalay in central Burma. Mandalay has a special place in the hearts of the Burmese, and remains a symbol of the proud days when Burmese kings ruled the country.

Today, Mandalay has a more contemporary look, because a 1980 fire leveled more than 6,000 buildings there. Still, the ancient "golden city" is revered by millions of Burmese, Buddhists, and foreign tourists, because it was the royal seat of the last two Burmese kings, Mindôn and Thibaw. King Mindôn founded Mandalay in 1857, to fulfill an ancient Buddhist prophecy. According to legend, Lord Buddha visited the sacred mount of Mandalay Hill long ago and prophesied that in the year 2400 of the Buddhist Era (CE 1857) a large city would be established at the foot of Mandalay Hill. King Mindôn fulfilled the prophecy and named the royal city Yadanabon, meaning "The City of Gems." The British renamed it Mandalay.

Kipling traveled in Burma but never set foot in Mandalay. However, his 1892 poem "Mandalay" gave many in the world outside of Burma their first glimpse of this exotic, isolated land. Kipling wrote poetically about the road to Mandalay in British Burma as a place "Where the flyin' fishes play, / An' the dawn comes up like thunder outer China 'crost the Bay!"

Another famous writer helped introduce the world to Burma as well: Eric A. Blair, better known as George Orwell. His powerful 1931 autobiographical essay "Shooting an Elephant," which he based on his experience as an officer in the British Imperial Police Force; his 1931 essay "A Hanging," which describes the execution of a criminal; and his 1934 novel *Burmese Days* are all set in Burma. Many scholars believe Orwell's experiences in Burma inspired even his most famous works, the anti-totalitarian books *Animal Farm* and *1984*, in which he wrote, "If you want a picture of the future, imagine a boot stamping on a human face—for ever."

Mandalay Hill

Burma's Diverse Ethnic Group

Burma is one of the most ethnically diverse countries in the world, with more than 130 distinct groups and more than one hundred different dialects and languages. Burma gets its name from the Buddhist Burman (or Bamar) people, and Burman is a term used to refer to the majority ethnic group. (Military generals renamed Burma the Union of Myanmar in 1989. However, the U.S. government has not adopted Myanmar as its English name.)

Historically, the Burman have lived in the country's central and upper plains, while clustered in the northeastern hills are the Shan, who comprise 9 percent of the population. The Karen, who have long fought against the Burmese junta, make up 7 percent. There are also the Rakhine people, who comprise 4 percent, the Chinese 3 percent, Indian 2 percent, and Mon 2 percent.

Civil strife, political upheaval, and economic stagnation in Burma have forced a significant number of ethnic groups to flee to neighboring countries. For example, 140,000 mostly Karen refugees live in remote camps in Thailand near the border. Another group, the Rohingya, has been refused citizenship by the Burmese government, and its people are considered illegal foreigners. The Rohingya, a Muslim group that numbers around 800,000, are prime targets for forced-labor drives by the junta. Hundreds of thousands have fled to Bangladesh, Malaysia, and Thailand. Yet another group, the Chin, are overwhelmingly American Baptists and live in the impoverished mountains near the India-Burma border. The Chin claim that the government persecutes its people because of their religious beliefs.

Buddhists make up 89 percent of Burma's population, while Christians make up only about 4 percent and Muslims 4 percent. Burmese law bars members of religious orders from running for public office. And members of Buddhist, Christian, and Hindu religious orders (such as nuns, priests, and monks) are barred from voting and joining political parties.

A map of the locations of the peoples of Burma within the country. The Karen people are located within the red areas.

General Aung San in London in 1947

THE ASSASSINATION OF AUNG SAN

Back in Europe, Great Britain had become fully entrenched in the war. It suffered from the relentless terror of Germany's air force, which carried out bombing blitzes from the skies that lasted for months. After the Japanese bombed the U.S. military base in Pearl Harbor, Hawaii, in December 1941, the United States joined the war and became Britain's chief ally. Although Britain valued Burma and its other colonies, fighting a war on multiple fronts spread its military and defense network thin, and far more important than the conflict in Asia was the struggle for Europe. This was to Burma's advantage—but also to Japan's, which had its own agenda.

By the time Japan bombed Pearl Harbor, the Thirty Heroes had amassed an army of thousands of Burmese. Known as the Burmese National Army (BNA), they fought behind the Japanese and chased the British out of Burma. Japan's military leadership named Aung San commander-in-chief of the BNA. Despite this title, ultimate power over the military was not vested in him; the Japanese had masterminded and led the attack against the British, and its leaders would hold the reins of power in Burma. Great Britain's retreat had not paved the way for Burmese independence, but actually for a second period of foreign occupation, this time by the Japanese. Aung San and other Burmese leaders had suspected that Japan might have ulterior motives, and their hunch proved disappointingly correct.

Hideki Tojo, the prime minister of Japan during most of World War II

"WE WILL FIGHT THE ENEMY"

In January 1943, Japan's prime minister, Hideki Tojo, announced that Burma would be given control over its government before the end of that year, and on August 1 its independence was granted. Aung San stepped down from his military post to become minister of defense and Ba Maw, a former prime minister during British occupation, was named prime minister. These titles, however, were empty. Japanese commander General Iida remained Burma's unchallenged leader.

This setup put Aung San in a difficult position. Japan had been vital to ridding Burma of the British, and Aung San was expected to be loyal to Japan, which he was—outwardly. He was leading a "double life, nurturing the independence movement while playing along with the Japanese" and Ba Maw. He followed Japanese orders about military policy, but all the while he was plotting a secret rebellion. Other Burmese military and political leaders were also making preparations for an uprising against the Japanese, and in August 1944 Aung San joined them to form the Anti-Fascist People's Freedom League (AFPFL). The association represented different political and ethnic groups from across Burma and was the first body that stood a chance to unify the country and overthrow its oppressors.

While Aung San and the AFPFL began making plans for the revolt, Allied troops, led by Britain and the U.S., were progressing in the war. In the European theater they were advancing on several fronts, and their troops in Asia were gaining ground, too, having encroached Burma's northern border in late 1944. Now it seemed that the AFPFL would have to ride—or suffer through—a wave of British-American victory against the Japanese.

Aung San and his comrades found themselves in a predicament: whether to side with their old oppressors, the British, in order to depose their new oppressors, the Japanese. Cooperating with the British might crush their hope for independence, for Britain might then reinstate its colonial government (still in exile in India) in Rangoon. There was also the risk that the British would charge Aung San and the other revolutionaries with treason for joining the Japanese in the first place.

From early 1945 onward things developed so rapidly that it was difficult for Aung San to coordinate with his command units in the AFPFL and the BNA. A tentative date for the uprising would be set, then changed, and then the strategy revised. The actual revolt was somewhat pre-empted when BNA commander Bo Ba Htu launched a maverick offensive against the Japanese, and another similar uprising quickly followed in western Burma.

Aung San's response to these mini-revolts was cunning. He assured the Japanese that the rest of the BNA remained loyal and that it was time for him to lead Burmese troops to the front and join the Japanese in the fight against the imperialists. His ploy worked, and in the keynote address at a send-off parade for his troops in Rangoon, Aung San publicly reiterated his loyalty: "Our army will fight for the benefit of the country. . . . We will fight the enemy with all the strength in our possession." Ba Maw and the

Aung San

Japanese applauded his allegiance, and the troops marched out of the city. What they failed to notice was that Aung San had been vague in his speech, not stating specifically whom he meant by "enemy." Ten days later it was too late—they realized that they were the enemy he had meant. Every division of the BNA turned on the Japanese. Aung San had launched the second revolt for Burmese independence in ten years.

The BNA held its own against the Japanese, and initially *Bogyoke* ("General") Aung San declined to make contact with his British counterparts. Many British officers and government leaders wanted him executed as a traitor, and Aung San feared that once in their hands he—and the revolution—stood little chance. Finally in May 1945 he agreed to meet with British commander Bill Slim, who promised Aung San's safety if the two met at Slim's headquarters. The two leaders came to an understanding, and the BNA joined forces with the British. Fighting in Burma continued, now with Aung San's forces coordinating with Slim's. On August 6 and 9 the U.S. dropped nuclear bombs on the Japanese cities of Hiroshima and Nagasaki, sealing the Allied victory over Japan. The next week Japan's Emperor Hirohito surrendered, and its military withdrew from Burma.

World War II left the British Empire in disarray. In London, the enormous tasks of reorganizing Europe and rebuilding Great Britain outweighed the question of what to do with British colonies. Still, Britain's colonial government-in-exile returned to Rangoon from India with something of a vengeance, and it appeared that the old ordering system might well resume where it had left off. Britain's governor-general of Burma, Reginald Dorman-Smith, accused Aung San of treachery and threatened to eliminate him from public life.

Fortunately, Aung San had gained favor with the Supreme Allied Commander in Southeast Asia, Lord Mountbatten, who was British. Lord Mountbatten recognized how esteemed Aung San was in the eyes of Burmese people and warned that the nation might rise up in revolt if its leader were arrested. He persuaded Governor Dorman-Smith not to prosecute the Bogyoke

A potter tries to tempt a shopper in Rangoon in 1945. British military and civil authorities worked to rehabilitate the city after the war.

and urged London leaders against doing so, too. Burma's most capable leader, Mountbatten held, was its greatest hope for a smooth transition to independence.

Shortly after Dorman-Smith resumed office, the government in London issued a document called the "White Paper" that outlined Burma's future. The White Paper promised Burma independence, but only after three years of continued British rule. Aung San felt this period was far too long, and he condoned protests against the White Paper and Dorman-Smith's mandate. After several months of strikes, the governor-general stepped down, and Britain's prime minister Clement Attlee recommended that the White Paper be revised to allow for a quicker transition to independence. On January 2, 1947, Aung San and other high-ranking Burmese leaders boarded a ship to London, where they were to negotiate the future of Burma with Prime Minister Attlee.

Prime Minister Attlee in 1945

Negotiations in London went well, and on January 17 Aung San and Prime Minister Attlee signed a treaty that laid out Burma's path toward independence. Within four months elections would be held, and within a year full sovereignty would be granted to a free Burmese government. Aung San returned home victorious and immediately took to the road to campaign on behalf of the AFPFL. The association had a strong following, and in the April elections its members won more than half of the seats to the Constituent Assembly, Burma's new representative legislature. The Bogyoke had united Burma, and it seemed the whole country was behind him in the march to independence.

ESCAPE TO PYAPON

By mid-June 1947 it appeared that life in Burma was turning for the better, if not back to normal. For the first few months after the national elections in April, Aung San had presided over the newly formed Constituent Assembly, which was busy drafting the country's constitution. He eventually relinquished his charge over the Assembly to U Nu, his colleague and old friend from university. No doubt the Bogyoke would continue playing a leading role in politics, but he also looked forward to spending more time with his wife Khin Kyi and their young family.

In the first few years of their marriage the couple had moved around Rangoon, and with Aung San frequently away from home, Khin Kyi was often alone in raising their two boys: Aung San Oo, born in 1943, and Aung San Lin, born a year later. During the war she and Aung San had often sheltered Burmese running from the Japanese occupation forces. Graceful and charming, yet bold and self-assured, Khin Kyi's love and support was indispensable to her husband's leadership and to their family.

In March 1945, just before BNA troops turned on the Japanese and Aung San launched the rebellion, it was Khin Kyi's turn to run and hide. Aung San could not go to battle and leave his wife—who was pregnant with their third child—and two young sons alone in Rangoon. On the night of March 18, five BNA soldiers arrived at the family's residence. Three of them were dressed in ragged civilian clothes, the other two as women pretending to be Khin Kyi's sisters. They were to escort Khin Kyi and her sons to Pyapon, a small town that would serve as their haven away from armed conflict in Rangoon.

The trip was difficult. They traveled by water in small, flat-bottomed riverboats called sampans, and along the way they encountered Japanese troops. When confronted about the purpose of her travel, Khin Kyi told the soldiers that she was taking her two sons to visit relatives in nearby Myaungmya. The farther away from Rangoon they moved, the more crowded the river became, and at one point they were even caught in the middle of attacks by Japanese aircraft.

Khin Kyi rode in sampans, flat-bottomed
boats similar to these.

As they neared Pyapon, they found the area flooded with Japanese soldiers. Fearing that the troops might become suspicious of Khin Kyi traveling so far from home without her husband, the group decided it was best to continue along the waterways toward a more inconspicuous fishing village.

Upon reaching the tiny hamlet, they were greeted on the dock by a lone Japanese soldier. He found it peculiar that a pregnant woman with two small children would travel to a tiny, remote village, but Khin Kyi laughed and coolly told him that she lived nearby and had been craving fresh fish. The soldier found this amusing, for he had come for the same reason. He welcomed them ashore. Though safe, Khin Kyi was anxious to hear news of the uprising. Rumors had begun spreading that Aung San was killed, but to Khin Kyi's joy a messenger arrived two weeks later with a handwritten note from Aung San, dispelling her worst fear. In the letter Aung San assured his wife and children that all was well and that victory was near at hand. On March 27 he had led the BNA in a surprise rear attack that crushed Japanese defenses, making it safe to return to Rangoon. That day has since been celebrated in Burma as Armed Forces Day, often symbolized by Aung San's picture.

This period of separation was one of the more trying times of their marriage, and upon Khin Kyi's return to Rangoon the couple looked forward to settling down, and to the birth of their third child. A few months later, on June 19, Aung San Suu Kyi was born—"Aung San," for her father; "Suu," for her father's mother; and "Kyi," for her mother. In Burmese, the meaning of the name is "bright collection of strange victories."

Tower Lane

Around this time Aung San moved the family into a turreted, colonial-style house on Tower Lane, near the center of Rangoon. After the Japanese surrendered and the British returned, the family was able to transition into a more comfortable, even normal, routine. Each morning, Aung San would leave for the office after breakfast with his wife and children. A private chauffeur would

Two-year-old Aung San Suu Kyi, center, with her parents
and two older brothers in 1947

drive him to work, one of the few luxuries he allowed himself.
He took advantage of the car ride to review important documents
and tend to other work-related matters.

The morning of July 19, 1947—two years and one month after
Suu Kyi was born—began as any other day would. Aung San
dressed in his traditional Burmese clothing: a silk jacket over a
collarless shirt and gold-colored pants, called lungi. The day on
which Burma would be granted full independence was rapidly
approaching, and he and the other cabinet ministers were busy
preparing for the transfer of power. After breakfast he kissed
Khin Kyi and hugged his children goodbye before setting off for
an important cabinet meeting.

At the same time that Aung San left his home for work, a
group of men armed with weapons left the residence of U Saw,
the former prime minister whom the British had banished to

Uganda for defying their authority. U Saw had not been included in the postwar negotiations concerning Burma's path to independence, nor in the provisional government that Aung San headed. He resented being left out and was outspokenly critical of the government and Aung San.

Though bearing guns, U Saw's hit men managed to evade security and gain entrance to the Secretariat building, where Aung San's meeting had just gotten under way. They climbed the stairs to the meeting room, burst open its doors, and stormed in. The cabinet members were caught off guard and completely defenseless against the armed intruders.

Chairs were overturned and bullets sprayed the room. Aung San was hit thirteen times and died instantly. In the old days of the Burmese kingdoms, one gained power by assassinating the ruler and claiming the throne. In Burmese this is known as "*thoke-thin-ye*," or "getting rid of one's rivals." Bitter and envious of Aung San's success, U Saw was determined to regain his position. He assumed that, by murdering Aung San, Burma's people would respect the thoke-thin-ye principle and recognize U Saw as the rightful successor. Even more, Britain might ask him to form a new government. On the contrary, the rule of law was enforced. The police followed a lead from a bystander at the Secretariat and traced the assassins' car plates to U Saw, who was arrested and sentenced to death. U Nu, one of the few leaders to survive the assassination, became prime minister.

Burma mourned Aung San's death. He had commanded the nation to victory over its enemy conquerors, becoming the beloved Bogyoke; he had negotiated independence from Great Britain and formed a government through elections, setting Burma on a path toward democracy; and he had united the country's different peoples, giving them hope for a shared and peaceful future. In his 1961 book, *The Union of Burma*, respected English historian Hugh Tinker commented that Burma's "admiration for Aung San is akin to worship." Aung San was the "father of Burmese independence." Such was his legacy, and the Burmese people were not quick to forget him.

Nowhere was the memory of Aung San more alive than at his family's home on Tower Lane. A flurry of activity continued about their house, with regular visits from Prime Minister Nu, other national leaders, and family friends. Khin Kyi constantly told her children about their father and reminded them of what he stood for. She hoped to set an example for them to follow. Though only a toddler at the time of Aung San's death, Suu Kyi developed a memory of her father—and gradually a feeling of responsibility to him and his cause. One of her earliest ambitions was to become a soldier. "Everyone referred to my father as Bogyoke . . . so I wanted to be a general too because I thought this was the best way to serve one's country, just like my father had done."

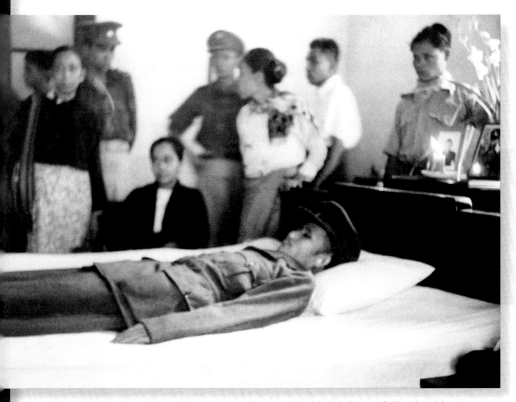

The body of General Aung San lies on a bed in his home following his assassination. Khin Kyi is seated behind the bed. An old Burmese proverb says, "One can't die if he's brave. Even when he dies his name lasts forever." This saying would prove true in the case of the General.

Prime Minister U Nu of Burma, front row, right, and his party pose in front of the Taj Mahal in 1960. Sitting, from left: Khin Kyi, Mrs. Sanwal, Mya Yi (wife of U Nu), and U Nu. Standing, B. D. Sanwal, commissioner of Agra, India, and S. R. Rao, superintendent of the government archaeological department in Agra.

LEAVING BURMA
FOR INDIA

After Aung San's assassination, the British government provided an annual pension of 100,000 Indian rupees to Khin Kyi, as well as to the families of the other assassinated ministers. This sum was nowhere near enough for her and her children to maintain their lifestyle. And because Aung San had retired from military service to take charge of the provisional government, his family was not entitled to the usual army pension. When the new Burmese government took full power, it might have extended Khin Kyi an offer of financial support, but she would have nothing of the sort. Determined to pull her weight, she would earn a living on her own.

Before marrying Aung San, Khin Kyi had worked as a nurse at the Rangoon General Hospital, so she made inquiries there about openings. When Prime Minister U Nu learned about this, he intervened—Khin Kyi deserved a job as befits the wife of Burma's former leader and national hero. He offered her a position as the director of the National Women and Children's Welfare Board. Khin Kyi thrived and quickly earned the title "Mother of Burma," a distinction formally bestowed in 1950 by the U.S. government.

Khin Kyi's work kept her busy, and her children often fell into the care of relatives and friends. In an interview with American author Whitney Stewart, Suu Kyi later recalled how much she enjoyed being read to when she was little, especially by her great aunt:

> [My great aunt] was always telling stories from
> the Jataka [tales of the early lives of the Buddha].
> She knew the whole story of the Buddha's life.
> Her knowledge of Buddhism was really very,
> very, broad, and she taught us a lot, especially
> me because she felt closer to me because I was a
> girl. I learned a lot about Buddhism the easy way.

Soon enough Suu Kyi took to reading on her own. She loved
Burmese and Western fairy tales, comic books, and especially
crime novels. She still remembers the day when a cousin brought
her a book by Arthur Conan Doyle, author of the Sherlock
Holmes mysteries. Suu Kyi devoured that book and all of Doyle's.
"How could Bugs Bunny's adventures compare with those of a
man who could, from a careful examination of a battered old
hat, gauge the physical and mental attributes, the financial situation, and the matrimonial difficulties of its erstwhile owner?"
she remembers thinking to herself. "I decided that detectives
were much more interesting and entertaining" than comic figures or cartoons. By the time she was thirteen, she also came to
love the classics.

Wherever Suu Kyi went, she brought a book with her, even
on shopping trips with her mother. One book in particular left a
lasting impression:

> The first autobiography I ever read was prov-
> identially, or prophetically, or perhaps both,
> *Seven Years Solitary*, by a Hungarian woman
> who had been in the wrong faction during the
> Communist Party purges of the early 1950s. At
> 13 years old, I was fascinated by the determi-
> nation and ingenuity with which one woman
> alone was able to keep her mind sharp and her
> spirit unbroken through the years when her only
> human contact was with men whose everyday
> preoccupation was to try to break her.

Although Suu Kyi was frequently in the company of her relatives and other elders, her mother was always around and served as a model of selflessness. One of Suu Kyi's favorite evening games was to walk around her mother's bed, and, each time she came full circle, to stop and pose a question. Even after a long day at work, Khin Kyi would return home and entertain her daughter's endless questions.

Unlike Aung San's mother, Khin Kyi did not over-indulge her children—one of the few toys Suu Kyi had was a doll that Aung San had bought for her in London. The doll was never treated as a plaything, but as a reminder of her father. As with most children, Suu Kyi initially felt that having a strict mother put her at a disadvantage. Only later would she look back and realize that her mother's discipline was rooted in love, and that it had prepared her to endure the trials she would face as an adult.

Also around were Suu Kyi's older brothers. She was closer to Aung San Lin than she was to their oldest brother, Aung San Oo, who did not care to play games and kept a distance from his younger siblings. Aung San Lin, on the other hand, was funny and boisterous. One of his favorite things to do was play pranks on friends and family. Suu Kyi delighted in his sense of adventure and had fun tagging along with him—though sometimes he was a little too daring and mischievous for her and for his own good.

One January morning while their mother was at work, Suu Kyi was outside playing with Aung San Lin. At one point she ran back inside the house for a few moments while Lin continued to play next to the pond beside their driveway. A toy pistol fell out of his pocket and bounced into the pond. Without hesitating he jumped in and retrieved the pistol, but one of his sandals got stuck in the mud at the bottom of the pool. He ran back into the house, gave his sister the toy gun, and then bolted back outside to retrieve his sandal. Some minutes later, his body was found floating face down in the middle of the pond. Lin's death devastated Suu Kyi. She had lost her brother and best friend. "I think in some way the death of my second brother affected me more than my father's death."

ACADEMIC LIFE

Shortly after Aung San Lin's death, the family moved into a new house on Inya Lake, near Rangoon University. Life there was just as vibrant as it had been on Tower Lane, if not more. Their home was a nexus of activity where prominent national leaders and normal Burmese alike intermingled. Suu Kyi's world view broadened tremendously from exposure to this socially diverse, multicultural community.

Khin Kyi emphasized to her children that it was important to respect everyone's beliefs—especially in Burma, where people from many different backgrounds lived together. "From my earliest childhood," Suu Kyi recalled, "my mother taught me this idea of national unity." On the nineteenth day of each month, Khin Kyi invited representatives from the Burman, Chin, Karen, Shan, Mon, and other ethnic groups to their home for a memorial service honoring Aung San. Bringing these groups together in the independence struggle had been one of Aung San's greatest achievements. The monthly service that Khin Kyi held was as much an occasion to honor Aung San as it was a time for the nation's leaders to come together and exchange their concerns and ideas.

A group of Karen people in 1968. The Karen people have a long history in Burma and make up 7 percent of the population.

While the family still lived at Tower Lane Suu Kyi had begun school at St. Francis Convent, a private, coeducational school in Rangoon where both of her brothers had also attended. It was there that she first began learning English, knowledge of which was considered essential to Burmese education and which served her well in the future. She excelled at St. Francis, earning top marks and a place at Methodist English High School, one of the best secondary schools in all of Burma.

The curriculum at Methodist English was bilingual (English and Burmese), and though the school was chartered by British Christian missionaries, its program and philosophy were ecumenical, striking a balance between Christian principles, Buddhist beliefs, and Burmese traditions. Given Suu Kyi's love of books, it came as no surprise to Khin Kyi that her daughter was drawn to subjects in the arts. But through firm resolve—at her mother's insistence—Suu Kyi eventually became a whiz in mathematics and science and rose to the top of her class in all subjects. She cherished the academic life at Methodist English as much as she did her social surroundings there. Among her peers at school were students from across Burma, including many sons and daughters of the nation's leaders in government, business, and the arts.

In Suu Kyi's tenth year of school, her mother was chosen by Prime Minister U Nu to be Burma's ambassador to India. India was one of Burma's closest allies, and the appointment was an honor and a remarkable opportunity for Khin Kyi. However, accepting the post meant taking Suu Kyi out of Methodist English and transferring her to a school in India (by then, Aung San Oo, Suu Kyi's older brother, had already left home to study in England). No longer would Suu Kyi live in a city where she went to market on Bogyoke Aung San Street and shopped at the huge Bogyoke Aung San Market. Still, the prospect of seeing the wider world excited Suu Kyi, and in late 1960 she and her mother set off for the bustling metropolis of New Delhi, India's capital. At the time, Suu Kyi assumed the move to India would be temporary—that she and her mother would return home to Rangoon at the end of her mother's post. Little did she know that when she left Rangoon, it would be twenty-eight years before she moved back to Burma.

Khin Kyi and Indian President Jawaharlal Nehru in 1960

LIFE IN INDIA

With a population rapidly approaching 1 billion people, India was the world's largest democracy when Khin Kyi and Suu Kyi arrived. The nation was transitioning out of a colonial system into an independent, free-market democracy, but not without turmoil— clashes and standoffs between the majority Hindus and the minority Muslims constantly disrupted progress. The Indian government was also struggling to mitigate widespread famine, which frequently caused food riots in poorer provinces.

At the international level, tensions between the globe's super- powers, the United States and the Soviet Union, were escalating, and the rest of the world was under pressure to step to one side or the other.

Burma and India remained close allies, in large part due to the friendship struck between President Nehru and Khin Kyi. President Nehru treated Khin Kyi especially well, offering her one of the finer diplomatic residences in New Delhi. He also introduced his two grandsons, Sanjay and Raji, to Suu Kyi, who had taken up horseback riding classes on the grounds of the Presidential Bodyguard. Suu Kyi had also begun lessons in piano and Japanese flower arrangement.

Suu Kyi's participation in these and other extracurricular activities was part of her mother's effort to make her daughter well rounded; but education remained the top priority. Suu Kyi completed high school at New Delhi's prestigious Convent of Jesus and Mary, a school for girls. After graduating she enrolled at Lady Shri Ram College, affiliated to Delhi University and considered India's premier institution of higher learning for women. At her mother's urging Suu Kyi studied political science, and in her courses she was introduced to the teachings of Mahatma Gandhi. Revolutionary leaders throughout the world would embrace Gandhi's philosophies of nonviolent resistance and satygraha ("force born out of truth"), and it was at Lady Shri Ram where Gandhi's ideals formed roots in Suu Kyi's mind.

Suu Kyi spent two years at Lady Shri Ram. Then, in 1964, she earned a place to study politics, philosophy, and economics at Oxford University in England. Khin Kyi was torn about her daughter's acceptance to Oxford. On the one hand, she had pounded into Suu Kyi's head the importance of education, and Oxford was one of the best universities in the world. On the other hand, Khin Kyi had lost her husband and one of her sons, and her other son was already away in England at school. Suu Kyi was her last child and family member still at home, and Khin Kyi feared that her daughter might forget about her and her heritage if she went away to the West.

Despite her reservations, Khin Kyi ultimately supported her daughter's decision to move to England and attend Oxford. The opportunity was simply too great. Plus, Suu Kyi would be near some of Khin Kyi's closest friends, the Gore-Booths. Paul Gore-Booth had been Britain's ambassador to Burma from 1953 to 1956, and he and his wife Patricia became acquainted with Khin Kyi through state events and social functions in Rangoon. The three friends then found each other again in New Delhi during Sir Gore-Booth's appointment as Britain's high commissioner in India, and it was there that their friendship blossomed. Khin Kyi developed a bond of trust and deep respect for the Gore-Booths, and it put her at ease to know that their house in London was a short ride from Oxford.

The main entrance of St. Hugh's College at
Oxford University

OXFORD, LONDON, LOVE & NEW YORK

Suu Kyi arrived at Oxford in 1964. The atmosphere there was similar to that at other university campuses in Europe and in the West. For youth of the postwar generation, it was a time of experimentation, sexual liberation, and protest.

On the whole Oxford students were not as radical as their counterparts at other European universities, but the general spirit of the age was certainly alive and evident on campus. Bands like the Beatles and the Rolling Stones were widely popular; males grew their hair long, females wore miniskirts; and some more daring students broke curfew and threw raucous parties on campus. Still, Oxford's academics remained quintessentially demanding and serious, and Suu Kyi very much took to the rigorous scholastic program there.

Suu Kyi was admitted to St. Hugh's College, one of five women's colleges in the university, and she took residence there for the duration of her studies. Being a woman, and one of only a few women from Southeast Asia, she stood out in the larger university community—all the more so because she usually wore the Burmese lungi: a close-fitting, ankle-length skirt that wraps around the body. Those who were not acquainted with her, and even many that were, knew her as "the daughter of some or other Burmese general."

If not for her father's renown, Suu's striking good looks made an immediate impression. In a memoir later published in Suu Kyi's book *Freedom from Fear*, one of her closest friends, Ann Pasternak Slater, wrote about being instantly captivated by Suu Kyi's beauty and her "inherited social grace." Suu Kyi was also known, if sometimes notorious, for her moral convictions. Some of her fellow students considered her values stiff and old-fashioned, but Pasternak Slater admired her for her sense of right and wrong.

Suu Kyi's manner and views at least partly resulted from growing up with her mother, whose insistence on being modest and womanly gave Suu Kyi a certain air of timidity and innocence. Her demeanor was also the product of her social surroundings. In addition to her schooling, Suu Kyi's social life had followed that of her diplomat mother's, which was very formal. Yet while Khin Kyi certainly had a significant influence over her daughter, Suu Kyi also arrived at her own personal convictions. For example, Suu Kyi told her female friends at Oxford that she intended to remain a virgin until she married—most certainly a Burmese man—and that she would remain faithful to him.

Like most intelligent young people, her curiosity sometimes caused Suu to let down her guard. In her second year at Oxford she decided that, at least once as a student, she would have to climb over St. Hugh's wall after curfew. Her accomplice was an Indian male student, and after the two ate a late meal he hoisted her back over the wall of St. Hugh's. Another time she resolved to try alcohol, which she did with two other girls in the bathroom at the university's Bodleian Library. Pasternak Slater offered an account of that episode:

> At the very end of her final year, in great secrecy, she bought a miniature bottle—of what? sherry? wine?—and, with two rather more worldly Indians as accoucheuses and handmaids at this rite of passage, retired to the ladies' lavatory in

the Bodleian Library. There, among the sinks
and the cubicles, in a setting deliberately chosen
to mirror the distastefulness of the experience,
she tried and rejected alcohol for ever.

While this may seem a tame, harmless experiment compared
to what many other college students were doing at the time, for
someone who had led a strictly disciplined life under public scru-
tiny, it was rather rebellious.

Margaret Stearn, a friend from St. Hugh's who went on to
become a respected British medical doctor, remembered how
being around Suu Kyi made one feel like a better person. "Suu
had the knack of putting one on one's best behaviour—not in a
restrictive sense, but in the sense of bringing out the best in you."
Similarly, Shankar Acharya, a classmate of Suu Kyi's who went
on to be a top adviser to the Indian government, was touched by
Suu Kyi's "unusual purity of mind and heart."

"Suu Burmese," as Pasternak Slater started calling her, made
an impression in other ways, too. She taught Pasternak Slater
and other friends from St. Hugh's how to eat rice with their fin-
gers and how Burmese women sit cross-legged on the floor, with
their lungi covering their legs. Her friends relished these cus-
toms and other insights into her culture, and in return they taught
Suu about English culture and some of its traditions. "She was
curious to experience the European and the alien," remembered
Pasternak Slater.

One English pastime that Suu Kyi especially enjoyed was
punting. It took many early morning training sessions for her to
get the hang of it, but she eventually mastered the art. Students
often recognized her atop a punt from great distances away
because of her trademark lungi. Active and athletic, Suu Kyi
also learned how to ride a bicycle, though the lungi was unsuited
for biking and it was then that she surrendered and bought her
first pair of jeans.

PUNTING

A punt is a long, narrow, flat-bottomed boat originally introduced in England as a fishing vessel. Punting for recreation only became widespread in the late nineteenth century, starting on the River Thames. From there the idea spread throughout England and became particularly popular in university towns like Oxford. A punt is difficult to operate on one's own and is suited only for shallow water. Its bow and stern are squared, and on one end is a platform on which the punter stands. Instead of rowing, as with a canoe, the punter propels the boat forward by pushing a long rod into the riverbed. Punts do not have rudders, which help prevent a boat from swerving off course, so the trick is to maneuver the punt forward without swinging around in circles. To keep a straight course, one must hug the pole tight against the punt while pushing, letting it swing like a rudder.

Other Oxford contemporaries remember Suu Kyi the academic. A fellow student in the politics, philosophy, and economics course, Robin Christopher, even claimed that Suu taught him "almost everything I know about economics . . . besides introducing me to the novels of Jane Austen—and me an Englishman!" One of her tutors at St. Hugh's, Julie Jack, praised Suu Kyi as being one of her sharpest students; but like most everyone else, Jack was also struck by Suu Kyi's composure and grace:

> My lasting impression of her is of a wholly composed, self-aware young woman: not in a calculated way, but in the manner of an instinctive thoroughbred. She was neither shy nor timid, as many others were during tutorials, but used herself sparingly. She dressed beautifully, sat beautifully, and walked beautifully.

Suu Kyi sat for her final examinations at Oxford in 1967. She had always earned top marks as a student, but surprisingly, her results were hardly exemplary. While researching for a biography about Suu Kyi, author Justin Wintle, an Oxford graduate himself, traveled to the university in 2005 and asked to view Suu Kyi's academic record. When he got hold of her results he started chuckling. "Is there something funny?" asked one of the librarians. Wintle explained that he was astonished to see that Suu Kyi had earned a third-class degree. "But you won't put that in your book, will you?" the librarian wondered. By that time Suu Kyi had become one of St. Hugh's most celebrated graduates, and the librarian feared for her reputation. "If I do," replied Wintle, "it will be out of respect for Aung San Suu Kyi's insistence on never concealing the truth."

In his biography Wintle went on to remind that many prominent individuals have done poorly on their final exams. J. R. R. Tolkien did worse than Suu Kyi, but he went on to become a distinguished professor at Oxford and write some of the twentieth century's most widely read books, *The Hobbit* and *The Lord of the Rings*. Suu Kyi, too, would not let a poor showing in her final exams take the wind out of her sails.

LONDON AND FINDING LOVE

After graduation Suu Kyi left Oxford for London, where she worked as a private tutor and a research assistant to Hugh Tinker, a professor at London University's School of Oriental and African Studies (SOAS). A decade earlier Professor Tinker had taught at Rangoon University and become acquainted with Suu Kyi's mother, as well as other friends of the family and leading figures in Burma. He went on to author a seminal book on Burmese history, but his knowledge extended into other fields as well. Suu Kyi was drawn to Professor Tinker's interest in her country, and she also took guidance from his leadership of organizations that dealt with nuclear disarmament and international race relations.

In London Suu Kyi was in good hands. She lived with the Gore-Booths, who furnished her with a small apartment that was separate from the rest of their house. They resided in London's upscale Chelsea district, and Suu Kyi was welcome to stay there indefinitely while she made plans for her future. They had introduced her to Professor Tinker, and through their other family connections Suu Kyi found herself in the company of some of London's most illustrious individuals. As they had promised Khin Kyi, the Gore-Booths made Suu Kyi a part of their family.

While still a student, Suu Kyi had spent semester breaks and holidays with the Gore-Booths, and she became good friends with their twin sons, David and Christopher. Like his father and Suu Kyi, David studied at Oxford; Christopher had opted to enroll at Durham University in northeastern England. As their parents had done, David and Christopher also introduced Suu Kyi to their friends, and through Christopher Suu Kyi got to know a young man named Michael Aris, a student at Durham.

Suu Kyi met Aris on a trip back to Chelsea before her Oxford finals, and at the time Aris was also preparing to sit for his exams at Durham. In the months after their graduation, Aris was a frequent guest at the Gore-Booth home. He developed an interest in Suu Kyi, and she found him attractive, too. Tall and handsome, he was also brilliant, and his serious, if quirky, interest in Tibet and the rest of the Himalayan region around Burma intrigued Suu Kyi.

Aris's passion for the culture and history of the Himalayan nations stemmed from his fascination with Buddhism, and his eccentric, exotic side derived at least in part from his upbringing. His father, John, held various appointments abroad in the service of the British Council, the nation's official cultural organization serving the world. Aris's mother, Josette, was the daughter of a French-Canadian emissary and also had an international background. She was a talented painter, and her passion for the arts corresponded well with John Aris's work at the British Council.

Michael Aris and his twin brother Anthony were born in Havana, Cuba, on March 27, 1946, nine months after Suu Kyi. The Aris family soon left Cuba for Peru, and after Peru they moved back to London, where they settled in Chelsea near the Gore-Booths. Aris attended the Worth School, a private boarding school in southern England that was similar to Suu Kyi's alma mater in Rangoon, Methodist English.

A memorable experience for young Michael Aris came when his father brought him a prayer wheel back from India, a gift purchased from a Tibetan exile. An inscription inside the wheel contained mysterious letters, and the message captivated Aris. He took the wheel to show his friends and teachers, and it happened that one of his teachers had studied the Tibetan language and could help Aris decrypt the message.

A Tibetan prayer wheel

This experience kindled Aris's interest in Tibetan culture and Buddhism, and though he studied modern history at university, he continued to occupy himself with anything related to Tibet that he could get his hands on.

To those who knew Suu Kyi and Aris in London, it came as no surprise that the two recent graduates developed an interest in each other; when they were together there was no mistaking their chemistry. Though they were happy, their relationship was just beginning, and both felt it needed to be drawn out before they made a commitment to each other. Plus, having just graduated from university, both of them had their own individual ambitions and neither wanted to enter marriage prematurely.

The test of their affection for one another came soon enough. Aris had captured the attention of Marco Pallis, a scholar, mountaineer, and musician. Pallis had lived and traveled extensively in Tibet and other regions of the Himalayas. By the time the two met, China had conquered Tibet and sealed it off to outsiders, especially to people from the West like Aris. Yet all hope was not lost. Through his contacts in the region, Pallis arranged for Michael to serve as an English teacher and tutor to the children of the royal family of Bhutan. He was to spend six years in their court. Though this seemed like a long time at the outset, the opportunity was too good to pass up, and Aris accepted.

Boys in the traditional Bhutanese dress (called *gho*)

Aris's immediate future lay in the East, not very far from Burma. Suu Kyi had already become restless in London, but she did not have her sights set on returning home yet. Not long after Aris's departure she was waving goodbye to the Gore-Booths and on her way farther west, across the Atlantic Ocean to New York.

For their relationship to endure the separation, Suu Kyi and Aris would have to write to each other—and this they did. By the time the two reunited in 1971 they had exchanged hundreds of letters. Through this correspondence they came to understand each other on a deeper level.

New York

Suu Kyi's research assistantship in London under Professor Tinker had kept her in touch with international affairs, particularly the situation in Burma. Although she enjoyed that work, even before she had begun she was already considering ways to put her degree to use in a more practical, humanitarian way. When the opportunity came to do graduate studies at New York University, Suu jumped at it, hoping this would open more doors for her. As in London, when she arrived in New York Suu Kyi quickly found herself in friendly and familiar company.

As far as her academics were concerned, Suu's mentor at New York University was Professor Frank N. Trager. Like Tinker, he had also worked in Rangoon and become acquainted with Khin Kyi and other friends of the family. And like Suu Kyi, his background and research interests spanned the fields of politics, economics, and philosophy. Between his research appointments and university posts, he had also served as an adviser to the United States on its relations with Southeast Asia, and his books on Marxism in that region and on the conflict in Vietnam received wide acclaim.

Suu Kyi's most important contact in New York, however, was Ma Than É, a beautiful, well-educated, and multitalented Burmese woman. She had studied at Rangoon University, only to leave school and enter teacher's training college, much like Khin Kyi. She had also earned a scholarship to study in England, and after finishing her academic program she became a famous singer of Burmese love songs.

Bogyoke Aung San and Khin Kyi had grown up listening to Ma Than's songs, and Aung San eventually met her in 1946. She was in London when Aung San brokered Burma's independence with Prime Minister Atlee, and she was invited to join the Burmese delegation at several dinners and events during the negotiations. Ma Than later became a member of the permanent staff of the newly formed United Nations organization, and in the mid-1960s she was on assignment in Algeria.

In 1965, on her first summer break from Oxford, Suu Kyi traveled to Algeria to stay with Ma Than, who had arranged for Suu to join one of the UN's humanitarian aid projects. Suu Kyi worked alongside other volunteers from around the world, and the post made a lasting impression on her. This opportunity was but a prelude to the experiences that awaited Suu when the two women reunited again.

Four years later Ma Than was back at the United Nations headquarters in New York. When she heard that Suu Kyi was coming to the city, she insisted that the Bogyoke's daughter live with her at her apartment near the UN campus. Although forty years separated them in age, the two became like family, and Suu lived with "Auntie Dora," as she often called Ma Than, for the remainder of her stay in New York.

New York City

Working at the United Nations

Suu began her postgraduate course at New York University in 1969, but after only a few weeks there she followed Ma Than's advice and applied to work at the United Nations. Several factors influenced her decision to postpone her graduate studies. In Ma Than she already had an advocate inside the UN, and by chance the UN secretary-general at the time was U Thant, one of Burma's most respected leaders and a well-regarded diplomat with influence in the international community.

After interviewing, Suu Kyi began the frustrating wait period while UN administrators completed the necessary background checks and profiling measures. Finally she was offered a job with the Advisory Committee on Administrative and Budgetary Questions. Her task was to oversee the finances of several agencies of the United Nations, including the UN Development Program and the World Health Organization. This position enabled her to apply what she had learned at university, and working at the United Nations, she witnessed firsthand how the world's foremost humanitarian and peacekeeping organization operated.

Her work kept her busy, but she always set aside some of her free time to volunteer at the Bellevue Center. Ma Than offered a portrait of the facility and Suu's involvement there:

> Staff members of the UN often devoted their evenings and weekends to voluntary aid activities. Bellevue is part of a large New York hospital. . . . It is mainly concerned with the city's poorest incurables and derelicts, who are brought in when life becomes too much for them, a temporary refuge for those on the verge of physical and mental collapse. Men and women are always needed to help with programmes of reading and companionship. Suu chose to volunteer many hours of her time every week for this. It was in the same tradition of service as her mother's.

Secretary-General U Thant in 1965

When not working or volunteering, she often attended events hosted by Secretary-General U Thant, who went out of his way to welcome Suu Kyi into his circle of friends. One such occasion came during Christmas of 1970. Suu Kyi, her old friend from Oxford, Robert Christopher, and two other officers in the British Foreign Service set out to sing Christmas carols to the secretary-general and some of his most senior associates. On the bus ride over to the performance the three young men got butterflies in their stomachs. Suu, on the other hand, kept her composure—she "always seemed to take things in stride," remembered Christopher. The ensemble was hardly professional, nor had they practiced, and in a moment of desperation they held a trial performance right there on the bus. Christopher later retold the story:

We decided that we should have a rehearsal on the way there, and that meant, to the amusement of other passengers, singing "Good King Wenceslas" on a public bus bowling along an ice-bound Third Avenue with Suu dressed in her finest Burmese costume. Fortunately, the Secretary General was similarly amused.

Sunday afternoons at U Thant's home were also pleasant. He hosted gatherings where guests were entertained and always treated to the finest Burmese food. Political talk was left at the door and the atmosphere was leisurely and convivial, a welcome break from the stress of work at the UN. Suu Kyi enjoyed U Thant's hospitality, especially the opportunity to mingle with Burmese expatriates and other foreign diplomats. She became acquainted with members of Burma's delegation to the UN, including U Soe Tin, its permanent representative. Like U Thant, U Soe Tin invited Suu Kyi and Ma Than to his home for dinners and parties.

During one session of the General Assembly, Suu Kyi and Ma Than heard that some of Burma's top-ranking officials wished to meet them. The two women happily accepted U Soe Tin's request to attend dinner, but Ma Than remembers feeling that "there was more to this invitation than met the eye." Her suspicion was confirmed when they arrived and saw that Colonel Lwen, a military man with no diplomatic ties, was also present at dinner. All of a sudden Suu Kyi found herself at the center of attention and the subject of an interrogation.

Colonel Lwen led Suu Kyi to an empty chair at the opposite end of the room from her aunt. No time was wasted; they immediately began questioning her. Why had Suu Kyi not surrendered the diplomatic passport she had been given when her mother was still ambassador to India? It was unlawful, the colonel told her, to hold it in her possession since her mother had resigned her post and retired. Colonel Lwen and many other Burmese military and government officials knew that Khin Kyi had stepped down because she did not want to be associated with Prime Minister Ne Win, Burma's dictator and Aung San's enemy. Further, he was suspicious of Suu Kyi's work at the UN. She might be using her position to undermine Ne Win's authority from the outside, and he was determined to uncover her real purpose for being in New York.

During the interrogation Suu Kyi remained calm and collected. She explained that her request for a regular passport had been properly placed with the Burmese Embassy, but that nothing had resulted. She would happily surrender her diplomatic

passport once the embassy issued her a new one. But she would not apologize for working at the United Nations or defend her political position to Colonel Lwen. Ma Than É claimed after the meeting that "being the daughter of General Aung San and Daw Khin Kyi," Suu Kyi "could not be taken down."

Quite contrary to the colonel's suspicions, Suu Kyi had little interest in returning to Rangoon for any great length of time, other than for a holiday or a visit with her mother; nor did she wish to meddle in the business of Ne Win's regime. She had other plans—with Michael Aris.

Fytche Square (now Mahabandula Garden) in Rangoon. Suu Kyi would not be returning immediately to her homeland.

Aris and Suu Kyi

chapter five

MARRIAGE AND MOTHERHOOD

In 1970 Aris left Bhutan to vacation in England, but not before visiting Suu Kyi in New York. Being apart had actually brought the young couple very close together, and Aris proposed marriage to her. She accepted gleefully, and the two began making plans for their wedding and their life together. Before their marriage they would remain apart, Aris in Bhutan and Suu Kyi in New York. A few months after becoming engaged, Suu traveled to Bhutan to visit Aris. He was thriving there, and Suu expressed her desire to move there and support him in finishing his assignment. They made plans to marry on Aris's next trip back to London, after which Suu would resign from the UN and join him in Bhutan.

The two were married in London on January 1, 1972. A service took place at the Gore-Booth home, and Buddhist ceremonies were carried out with a small group of friends and family present. Following tradition, guests were invited to wind the white string of connection to the Buddha around the young couple as they sat on the floor of the drawing room. After the service there was a reception at a nearby hotel, with the Gore-Booths serving as hosts. Aris's father and stepmother were supportive and entertaining, too, and they even dressed in traditional Bhutanese regalia.

Sadly, neither Suu's brother Aung San Oo nor her mother came to the wedding. Khin Kyi was let down. She did not understand how her daughter could marry an Englishman after all the years Aung San had fought against British colonial rule. Khin Kyi wondered whether her daughter had forsaken her family and her homeland.

Khin Kyi eventually changed her mind after meeting Aris, finding him winsome and kind. She could tell that he and Suu Kyi were in love, and she was happy that they were together.

Suu Kyi was forgiving of her mother's initial reaction, but she feared that other Burmese would not be so quick to change their minds. Many of them were already irritated—some even hostile—because she had left Burma, and her marriage to Aris only aggravated them even more. In the months leading up to their marriage, she often brought up in her letters to Aris the subject of her responsibility to Burma. Although she had been away for some years, she had not ruled out the possibility, even the necessity, of returning one day:

> I only ask one thing, that should my people need me, you [Michael] would help me to do my duty by them. Would you mind very much should such a situation ever arise? How probable it is I do not know, but the possibility is there. Sometimes I am beset by fears that circumstances and national considerations might tear us apart just when we are so happy in each other that separation would be a torment. And yet . . . I am sure love and compassion will triumph in the end.

Aris promised to stand by her side, not sure what the future would bring, but knowing full well that he had not simply married "the daughter of some or other Burmese general," but "the daughter of the father of Burma."

In their first year of marriage Aris and Suu Kyi lived in Thimphu, the capital of Bhutan. Aris continued tutoring the royal children, and having mastered the Bhutanese language, Dzongha, he was often called upon to translate important texts and other government documents into English. He had developed a friendly rapport with his hosts, who treated him as one of their own and even furnished him with a small house. When not tutoring or translating, he spent considerable time studying the country's history. His position afforded him access to libraries, museums, and other cultural and religious institutions, and these facilities provided him with tremendous resources for cultivating his research.

In Suu Kyi's words Bhutan ("Land of the Thunder Dragon") was "a tiny and remote kingdom barely known to foreigners— a country of lovely, peaceful Himalayan valleys, huge medieval fortresses and handsome people clad in traditional, hand-woven robes." With most of its population concentrated in Thimphu, the rest of the country was ripe for exploration, and in their free time Aris and Suu enjoyed long hikes. Their favorite areas were the valleys between the three parallel mountain ranges running north to south. As long as one remembered one valley from the next, and did not veer off course up a mountain, it was impossible to get lost.

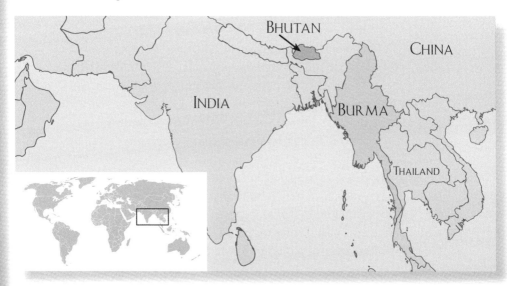

Bhutan is located northwest of Burma.

On one such two-day hike with Aris, Suu Kyi longed for a shower or a bath. As was the custom in these villages, local dwellers led her to a hollowed-out tree trunk lying on the ground in full view of the village. The water was heated by hot stones, but she balked at bathing in front of so many people. Only after Aris persuaded some villagers to help him erect grass screens around the tree trunk was Suu Kyi willing to bathe, and even then only in her undergarments. Such modesty was uncommon in Bhutan, but Suu Kyi had found a way to join in on the fun of exploring these remote areas without compromising her sense of decency.

Suu Kyi did not spend all of her time exploring Bhutan's valleys. She put her experience and practical knowledge to work by advising the Bhutanese government. Bhutan had recently joined the United Nations, and she became a consultant on UN relations at the foreign ministry. She had a knack for making the most of her circumstances, a trait that served her well in the future as she transitioned between cities, raised a family, and furthered her own career.

HOPSCOTCHING FROM COUNTRY TO COUNTRY

As Aris's post to the royal court neared an end, he and Suu Kyi began making plans for their next move. They had enjoyed their time in Bhutan, but they felt that their future, at least their immediate future, lay outside of the Himalayas. They had their own individual aspirations, but the two reached decisions about their future together, and with their next move, as with their first, Aris's career would take precedence. With his research Aris had laid the foundation for a doctoral dissertation, and it was a career in academia that he wanted. Suu was happy to follow, especially since the couple received news that she was pregnant with their first child.

Aris and Suu Kyi returned to London just before Christmas in 1972. Aris had been accepted to the doctoral program at the School of Oriental and African Studies (SOAS), where Suu Kyi had researched under Professor Hugh Tinker before moving to New York. His adviser would be Professor Hugh Richardson, a well-known scholar of Tibetan studies. With a baby boy on the way, living in London was also favorable because Aris's family, and Suu's guardians, the Gore-Booths, would be around. Their son, Alexander Myint San Aung Aris, was born at the Queen Charlotte Hospital in April 1973.

Aris's family helped them buy a small apartment in London, one that their friends would later remember as being white, tidy, and meagerly furnished. But after just a few months there, and only weeks after Alexander was born, another move was already on the horizon. They would be going back to Southeast Asia, this time to Nepal, where Aris would lead an expedition to Kutang and Nubri funded by the University of California. This continual hop-scotching from country to country, from project to project, marked their first years together. While in Nepal they visited Suu Kyi's mother in Burma. This was the first time that Khin Kyi met Aris, and he and baby Alex won her affection immediately. She renounced any misgivings she had about Suu Kyi's marriage to a Briton and took joy in her daughter's happy union and family.

Suu Kyi, Aris, and Alex returned to England at the end of 1974, staying briefly in London before retreating to Grantown-on-Spey, Scotland. Their flat in London had been too small for the three of them, and Aris was not bound to SOAS. This sleepy town in the Scottish Highlands was not chosen at random, for Aris's father and stepmother, John and Evelyn Aris, had bought a home there in advance of John's retirement.

Following the pattern they had set since Bhutan, the couple moved yet again after less than two years in Grantown. Aris's dissertation was developing well, and his work had created something of a buzz in the field of Southeast Asian studies. His progress was confirmed, and propelled, when Oxford University offered him a research fellowship at St. John's College. Once again, Suu Kyi was delighted to follow Aris. In Grantown she had taken part in community activities, even joining a dressmaking class with a neighbor of hers, but living in Oxford would afford her opportunities within the university community—perhaps to sit for another degree, or even to write a book.

BACK IN OXFORD

A year after the family moved to Oxford, Suu Kyi gave birth to their second son, Kim Htein Lin Aris, on September 24, 1977. Kim was named after the hero in a novel of the same name by Rudyard Kipling.

Suu Kyi was intent on instilling in her sons the same values that her mother had taught her, and that meant being a loving, but strict, mother. She also taught Alex and Kim about Burmese traditions so that they would understand their mother's heritage. Wherever they lived—Nepal, Bhutan, Scotland, England—she found ways to carry on these traditions, and it helped that a constant stream of family and friends from Burma were guests at their home in Oxford.

After Kim was born the family moved from their small flat on the grounds of St. John's College to a larger house in north Oxford, not far from St. Hugh's where Suu had lived as a student. There, in true Burmese fashion, they could "welcome and uncomplainingly entertain for punishing periods" Suu Kyi's relatives and the couple's other friends from Southeast Asia. These visits were a welcome reminder of life back home, but in England, Aris's family was quite generous and loving toward Suu Kyi as well. She and the boys were always welcome in their home, and both families often vacationed together.

St. John's College, Oxford

Suu was grateful for the Arises' hospitality and often went to great lengths to return their favor. On one occasion she prepared Peking duck, and the story remains a legend in Aris family lore. In Burma, Peking duck "required a wind-dried, glazed finish." Not one to cut corners, and ever enterprising, Suu Kyi achieved the desired result by enlisting every member of the household to take turns applying a hair dryer to the meat while she finished preparing the rest of the meal.

The responsibilities of raising two children and caring for her family kept Suu Kyi quite busy, but she did not complain. The family was on a tight budget until Aris finished his dissertation, but Suu made the most of what they had. She washed dirty laundry, cooked meals from scratch, and even made clothes, taking to her role as wife and mother with typical vigor. Somehow she still managed to set aside some time for herself, made easier once the boys grew older. With them in school and Aris busy editing a volume of essays on Tibet, Suu Kyi took a part-time job at Oxford's Bodleian Library. Charged with organizing and sourcing new material for its Burmese collection, she routinely made trips back to Rangoon. This invariably meant visiting her mother, but Suu also connected with several people who would help revive her interest in Burma.

One of these contacts was U Tin Moe, a professor of Burmese literature at Rangoon University. An adversary of Ne Win, "Uncle" Tin Moe would often implore her to help Burma. He never specified how she might serve, but his nudging had its intended effect—turning her attention back on the situation at home. He also made a considerable contribution to Suu Kyi's project at the Bodleian Library by shipping Burmese classics to her in England. Professor Tin Moe was later arrested and tortured by Burma's military regime, but he managed to escape to Thailand and live there in exile.

Burma's ever-present military soldiers at the Shan State Kalaw
market during heavy monsoon rains

Along with taking care of her family and working at the library, Suu Kyi also started writing. Ever since she could read she had wanted to become a writer, an aspiration she shared with her father. She applied for a second bachelor's degree in English literature, but Oxford rejected her application. Not one to be let down by failure, she turned her energy to writing a biography of her father, for which she built up an impressive collection of books about Burma and its history. She also began learning Japanese, as her father's dealings with the Japanese represented a crucial period in his life and the nation's history. Out of her research came plans for a doctoral thesis in Burmese political history, which she intended to take up at SOAS. Again, she was denied admission, perhaps because of her sub-par results at university. In the meantime she wrote a trio of short guides to countries she knew from experience: *Let's Visit Burma*, *Let's Visit Bhutan*, and *Let's Visit Nepal*, all published in 1985.

That same year she applied a third time for another degree. It had been suggested that she focus on Burmese literature, and this time, SOAS admitted her to its doctoral program. She sat for language exams that tested her proficiency in Burmese, and she aced them. She had lived outside of Burma for twenty-five years, but her review panel was amazed to find that her Burmese had survived with barely a discernible blemish. At SOAS doors began to open for her. She received an eight-month research scholarship to study at the Center for Southeast Asian Studies (CSEAS) at Kyoto University in Japan.

Once again the family was on the move, but this time they would be separated. Michael, now Dr. Aris, had also won a fellowship, to the Institute of Advanced Studies in Simla, India. Alexander was at boarding school in England, but Kim was only eight and too young to be away from his parents. He would go to Japan with his mother. He could attend school there, and Suu Kyi expected that they would learn Japanese in no time. She turned the family bathroom into a language center—everywhere Kim or Suu Kyi might look, Japanese characters were taped to the walls and fixtures.

KYOTO AND SIMLA

Kyoto is one of Japan's most beautiful cities. Nestled in the Yamashiro Basin with mountains on three sides, it was not a target of Allied bombings during World War II. Many of its old shrines and temples are designated World Heritage Sites by the United Nations, and Kyoto University ranks among the finest in the world. At the center of the city are the magnificent Imperial Park and Palace, home to Japan's emperors until the late nineteenth century, when the royal court moved to the new capital, Tokyo.

With Kim at her side, Suu Kyi often rode the *shinkansen*, or bullet train, to Tokyo, where she interviewed soldiers who had known her father during the Japanese occupation of Burma. Traveling at breakneck speeds, on these and other trips, they

took in the country's varying landscapes and rich culture. One of Suu's hobbies was cooking, and she especially enjoyed sampling Japanese dishes and learning how to prepare them. During her time there she made substantial progress in researching for her dissertation and learned a great deal about her father's involvement with the Japanese.

At the end of her fellowship, Suu Kyi traveled with Kim to spend three months in Rangoon with her mother, before moving on to Simla to be with Aris. Simla lies at the foot of the Himalayas, about two hundred miles north of New Delhi. Often called the "Queen of the Hills," it was established as a hill station in the mid-nineteenth century. A hill station is a town built above a valley or low-lying plain, and these settlements cropped

The Imperial Palace and gardens in Kyoto, Japan

up across India during colonial times. In the summer, temperatures in hill towns were much cooler than in the valleys below. The hill station at Simla served as the capital of the colonial government during the summer months, when the British found New Delhi insufferably hot.

Aris secured a one-year fellowship for Suu Kyi at the Institute for Advanced Studies where he was working. She wrote two essays about Burma: "Literature and Nationalism in Burma" appeared in print in 1987, and three years later the Simla Institute published the more notable "Intellectual Life in Burma under Colonialism." She argued that Indian leaders like Gandhi and Prime Minister Nehru, whom she had met, had attained prominence in the world because they "were able to use the English language to make their views known to the world. Because they handle the western intellectual idiom so masterfully, the world regarded their views as worthy of serious consideration." The voices of Burmese leaders and intellectuals, on the other hand, had not reached the wider world, despite the country's vibrant intellectual and literary scene. Suu Kyi alludes to the question of whether Burma would, or could, produce an ambassador to the world, a voice that could be heard across the globe and not overshadowed by the country's problems—or censored by its government.

In the summer of 1987 Suu Kyi and Aris waved goodbye to Simla and returned to Oxford. Suu had made substantial progress toward completing her dissertation, and in England she traveled back and forth between Oxford and London for research and consultation with her advisers. Aris, now a tutor at Wolfson College, was becoming a respected authority on Tibetan studies, and Suu was well on her way to joining him in the ranks of academia. Life for the family was speeding up, too. They settled into a spacious house in Oxford, renting the top floors to tenants and frequently sharing their own quarters with family or guests from out of town. With the boys older and Aris earning a professor's salary, circumstances were favorable for Suu to devote more time to her interests.

Ann Pasternak Slater was also in Oxford at the time, and her mother, the sister of Russian novelist Boris Pasternak, author of *Doctor Zhivago*, lived in Suu's neighborhood. On visits to her mother's home, she would meet Suu for walks around their neighborhood or for afternoon tea. Suu relished having more time at her disposal, but Ann remembers her feeling "dissatisfied with a life that failed fully to engage her energies, her relentless determination, the inherited diplomatic and political skills she had just begun to feel burgeoning during her years at the United Nations." Ann's mother eventually fell ill, and Suu often visited her at home, being "one of the few she welcomed, a serene presence at her side."

Not long after the elderly Mrs. Pasternak Slater became sick, Suu received an urgent call from halfway around the world, informing her that her own mother was in critical condition at Rangoon Hospital. Looking back on that night, Aris wrote:

> It was a quiet evening in Oxford like many others, the last day of March 1988. Our sons were already in bed and we were reading when the telephone rang. Suu picked up the phone to learn that her mother had suffered a severe stroke. She put the phone down and at once started to pack. I had a premonition that our lives would change forever.

Though they could not foresee it at the time, Aris's intuition was spot-on.

A view of Sule Pagoda Road and the
Sule Pagoda in Rangoon

RETURNING TO BURMA

Suu Kyi arrived in Rangoon on April 2, 1988, and rushed to Rangoon General Hospital to be at her mother's side. The stroke had immobilized *Daw* (literally "aunt") Khin Kyi, but her mental faculties were still intact. Suu Kyi essentially took up residence at the hospital, going to her mother's house only to change clothes and pick up mail. Although her attention was fixed on caring for her mother, she could not help but notice that there were a surprising number of young patients being treated at the hospital. Soon enough she learned that they were students recovering from injuries sustained in confrontations with military and police forces.

Demonstrations had rocked the capital since autumn of the previous year. On September 5, 1987, the people of Burma awoke to discover that General Ne Win, head of state and commander of the military, had introduced monetary and financial reforms that effectively robbed them. Their old bank notes were declared illegal tender, meaning they could not be used as cash for payment. This sudden change proved a setback for students in particular because the announcement came just as they were required to pay tuition fees and other dues for the coming year.

On the day that monetary reforms entered effect, hundreds of outraged students from Rangoon University sabotaged government buildings and wrecked other public property in the north of the city. The military government had anticipated a backlash and quickly moved to restore order in the capital. Universities and colleges across Burma were shut down, but when they reopened six weeks later, students again responded with protests. After a few small outbursts of violence, military and police forces crushed the student uprising with use of force. Confrontations between students and the military police continued until the spring of 1988, culminating with a mass demonstration and a military crackdown in March 1988 that left hundreds of students dead and many more injured.

Students attempt to overturn a truck during riots
in Rangoon, Burma, on March 20, 1988.

Manipulated and Exploited

Military use of force was not new to Burma. After a brief period of democratic rule under Prime Minister U Nu (following Aung San's assassination in 1947), General Ne Win had seized power in 1962 through a military coup d'état. Immediately following his putsch, Ne Win suspended the constitution and gradually tightened his grip over the nation and its resources. He closed off the country from the outside world, banishing foreign journalists and taking control of the Burmese press. He requisitioned industries, nationalized Burma's banks, and established a one-party police state that came to be based on repression and terror.

In a matter of a few years after the military takeover, General Ne Win's dictatorship had cemented, and the nation bore no resemblance to what Aung San and the Thirty Heroes had envisioned and fought for. Worse still, Ne Win himself had been a "Hero." Suu Kyi's mother, Daw Khin Kyi, resigned her ambassadorial post in India in 1967 for the very reason that she did not wish to be associated with the military regime.

Ne Win satisfied his enormous lust for power with policies that ruined Burma's economy. A hard line, he claimed, was necessary in order to fight off insurgent groups. These forces, he argued, posed a dangerous threat to the country's stability and prosperity. By the mid-1970s most of Burma's mountainous areas were controlled by warlords who commanded their own armed militias.

The strongest and wealthiest of these groups were the Communist Party of Burma (CPB) and the Karen National Union (KNU). These and other forces funded their armies through profits from the narcotics trade. On Ne Win's watch Burma became one of the world's largest producers and exporters of opium, which he seemed to turn a blind eye to. Heroin from Burma earned a reputation for being some of the world's purest and was sold on the streets of major cities in the West, including the United States. Opium poppy fields colored areas near the Chinese, Thai, and Laotian borders, and smuggling into these countries was relatively easy.

Insurgents across the country were engaged in perpetual battle with each other, and Ne Win's corruption and battle-mongering seemed only to abet these mini civil wars. With renegade factions constantly beating each other up, Ne Win's authority was secure so long as no one group became powerful enough to compete with his military.

Aware of his unpopularity, Ne Win sometimes appeased the people by pretending to loosen his grip on power. One such deceptive act came in 1971, when he announced his resignation from the military. He and twenty other freshly retired military officers formed a "civilian" committee to draft a new constitution, something the citizens of Burma had wanted. A referendum, or vote, on the proposed constitution would be held and Ne Win encouraged people to turn out and vote. On the day of the referendum in December 1973, instructions were simple: place a "yes" vote in the white box and a "no" vote in the black box. But voting was not carried out in secret—armed members of the Tatmadaw (Burma's armed forces) stood guard at the polls and monitored how each person voted.

To no one's surprise, Ne Win's proposed constitution passed, with more than 90 percent of votes cast in favor. It entered effect in 1974, but not much changed. Ne Win became chairman of the Burma Socialist Program Party (BSPP), which had drafted the constitution. No elections were scheduled for the future, and no other parties were allowed to form. Under this one-party system, Ne Win retained absolute power, and the military remained at his disposal.

By the mid-1980s the people of Burma were accustomed to being manipulated and exploited, and when Suu Kyi arrived in Rangoon in the spring of 1988, she found her nation on the verge of a humanitarian crisis. The production of rice, Burma's main crop and a staple in the Burmese diet, had already fallen to abysmally low levels, and other food shortages were endemic, too. On top of that, gasoline and essential medications were in equally short supply.

With the demonetization of September 1987, not only was rice and other food scarce, but the majority of the population barely had money for purchasing essential goods and provisions. A land that formerly had been one of the richest in Southeast Asia was now a "Least Developed Country" according to the United Nations, and one of the ten poorest nations in the world.

Over the years Suu Kyi had heard from afar about what was happening in Burma, but on trips back her contact had been mostly with friends and family. This left her somewhat in the dark about her homeland's predicament. Now, at her mother's side in Rangoon Hospital, she began hearing stories that shed light on Burma's problems. She learned that the latest wave of violence in Rangoon had surged in the second week of March, just a fortnight before her arrival in town.

Daily life in Rangoon in 1987

STUDENT RALLY TURNS DEADLY

The impetus for that violence had been a fight between students at Rangoon's Institute of Technology and some local men, taking place on March 12 at the Sanda Win tea shop near the campus of the Institute. There are various explanations for how the brawl started, but that one of the students, Win Myint, was stabbed is indisputable. Eventually the police arrived on the scene and made arrests. The students took Win Myint to the hospital on campus, where he explained to everyone what had happened. After some time the men who had instigated the fight—including Win Myint's attacker—were released by government authorities. Students protested the government's impunity toward Win Myint's assailant and gathered in front of the Sanda Win shop to demand that justice be served. The government responded by dispatching its armed riot police, known as the Lon Htein, to maintain order. A crowd gathered, and when the mob refused to disband, the police opened fire. A violent clash ensued, and one student, Maung Phone Maw, was killed.

The Sanda Win shop incident and Maung Phone Maw's death outraged students at the Institute, but they refused to stoop to violence. They organized a peaceful march on the evening after their friend had been shot, and in subsequent days they held rallies on campus. On March 15, the Lon Htein broke up their rally and warned against any further anti-government demonstrations. Students at the Institute refused to back down, and the next day their counterparts at Rangoon University joined them in a peaceful march that wound along the bank of Lake Inya, which separates the campuses of both schools.

While trying to cross from one side of the lake to the other via the White Bridge, the band of students came upon a troop of Lon

Burmese soldiers clear the streets during a
pro-democracy rally in Rangoon in 1988.

Htein on the other side of the bridge; the police troop was stationed there to prevent the march from continuing. Three student leaders stepped forward to reason with the soldiers and request permission to proceed. After several minutes, they came back to report that the police had forbidden them from marching on.

The students were committed to a peaceful march and agreed to retreat rather than clash with police. On turning around and starting back across the bridge, they realized that a separate contingent of Lon Htein had maneuvered to the other side; they were trapped on the bridge. Some students jumped into the lake and swam to safety, but many were not so lucky. The police mounted a charge from both sides, capturing students and slaughtering them on the spot. The soldiers did not fire their weapons, but they clubbed the male students and even dragged some of the female students to the water, where they were raped and drowned by hand. Most accounts estimated that several hundred students died.

James Mawdsley, a British journalist and human rights activist, happened to be on hand at the Inya Lake protest. The Lon Htein spared his life, but the Burmese government arrested him for participating. His imprisonment lasted fifteen months and made news worldwide. He was finally deported and later wrote about his incarceration and the events he witnessed in *The Heart Must Break*. In his accounts of the violence at Inya Lake, he spared no details:

> What horrifies me every time is trying to imagine a man who is fit, strong, well-armed and surrounded by colleagues, who is backed up as well by one of the world's largest armies, charging after hapless young girls and clubbing them to death. What is he thinking as he smashes his baton into her face? When she screams in the water and goes under does he reach down to pull her up by the hair so he can break her skull? She will not die with one or two blows. He must hit her on the arms and back and chest before getting a few good shots in at her face.

The following day, authorities ordered that the bridge be cleaned to remove the bloodstains. From that point on, the White Bridge symbolized the tragedy of what was meant to be a peaceful protest. It became referred to as the Red Bridge, and the massacre of that day, "White Bridge, Red Bridge."

After White Bridge, Red Bridge the government shut down as many roads and meeting points as possible. It closed doors to schools and universities, hoping to suppress the unrest by targeting students, the driving force behind resistance protests. Rangoon General Hospital was one of the few places the government did not shut down, and its rooms and corridors became filled with visitors, patients, doctors, and other staff talking discreetly about what was happening.

Such was the mood at the hospital when Suu Kyi arrived in April. At first, her presence there went unnoticed; she observed what was happening and listened to what was said, but kept to herself. Soon enough, however, it leaked that Aung San's daughter was staying at the hospital. She started asking questions and listening in earnest, but refrained from speaking out. Her inquisitiveness and readiness to listen gave the impression that she was willing to help. She had always planned to give back to her country by establishing libraries and scholarship programs for students; but more than philanthropy, Burma needed fundamental change.

Demonstrations continued across the nation and often escalated into violence. Textile factory workers showed their solidarity with student protesters and walked off their jobs. After being open again for a short period, Rangoon University's campus was once again sealed off by the Lon Htein on the evening of June 20. Students met there to protest, and when the Lon Htein attacked, the students retaliated with jinglees—slingshots that fire sharpened bicycle spokes.

By July of 1988 even Buddhist monks had become involved in the peaceful rallies, joining in the spirit of engaged Buddhism, a doctrine whereby Buddhist beliefs are put into practice in order to effect social, political, or economic change.

A HOME, A HEADQUARTERS

As Suu Kyi watched Burma spiral further into chaos, she also witnessed her mother's health deteriorate drastically. Daw Khin Kyi's condition had not improved since suffering the stroke. She showed little sign of recovering, and doctors informed Suu Kyi that her mother was dying. Suu decided to remove her mother from the hospital and take her to No. 54 University Avenue, the family home for several decades. For her mother she arranged the nicest room downstairs, one with a view overlooking the lovely garden that Khin Kyi had tended for so many years. A cook and two maids, living in the servants' quarters on the premises, ensured that Daw Khin Kyi received constant care, but Suu Kyi remained her mother's principal caretaker.

The house at No. 54 was large enough to serve as an infirmary for Khin Kyi and as a makeshift headquarters for the burgeoning democracy movement that was gravitating around Suu Kyi.

Suu Kyi's home at No. 54 University Avenue

It was in this setting that Aris, Alexander, and Kim arrived in the summer of 1988 once the school year had ended in England. In his introduction to *Freedom from Fear*, Aris described the atmosphere there:

> Suu's house quickly became the main centre of political activity in the country and the scene of continuous comings and goings as the curfew allowed. Every conceivable type of activist from all walks of life and all generations poured in. Suu talked to them all about human rights, an expression which had little currency in Burma till then.

The young activists had first met Suu at the hospital after the March violence. They were drawn as much to the flurry of activity at the house on University Avenue as they were to Suu Kyi's persona, a model to them of service, grace, and vigilance. Tin Hlaing called Suu Kyi "a second mother, sometimes scolding me to keep my clothes tidy, but sometimes, if her busy schedule permitted, washing them for me herself."

There were also writers, lawyers, doctors, artists, and other intellectuals, many of whom were close friends of Khin Kyi and came to be with her as she lay ill. But most significant of all were the retired military officers who had fought with Suu Kyi's father in the independence struggle decades before. These men held close the memory of Aung San, having served him, and subsequently U Nu, during the period of democracy. That Burma had not become the country they and the Bogyoke had once envisioned disgruntled them, and they were eager to join Suu Kyi in reclaiming Burma.

Among those old military friends of Aung San who became regular guests at No. 54 was U Tin Oo (also spelled U Tin U), a retired general. He had joined the Bogyoke's army in 1943, fought against the Japanese, and risen to become a high-ranking officer in Ne Win's Revolutionary Council. Under U Nu he had been well regarded by the people of Burma. His popularity unsettled Ne Win, who eventually stripped Tin Oo of his rank and sentenced him to prison on charges of sedition. This was one of the ways that Ne Win had consolidated power early on— by purging leaders who threatened his authority. U Kyi Maung was another friend of Aung San whose military and political career Ne Win terminated. Kyi Maung had risen to the rank of regional commander, but his public criticism of Ne Win's coup d'etat in 1962 cost him a prison sentence. Other early opponents of Ne Win, such as Aung Shwe, avoided banishment to prison by accepting diplomatic assignments overseas, where they were considered less of a threat. There was also U Lwin, who briefly had served as deputy prime minister under Ne Win until 1980, when he resigned in protest of the junta.

These military officers and other seasoned leaders visiting No. 54 urged Suu Kyi to step forward and take command of the movement for democracy. Suu Kyi's commitment to their ideals was undisputed, but she was hesitant to take an active stance. At that point she had no intention of forming a political party or in joining any of the revolutionary parties that were militant.

Two pivotal events would change her mind. The first was Ne Win's announcement in late July that he would resign as prime minister and army chief. He accepted part of the blame for Burma's collapse:

> As I consider that I am not totally free from responsibility, even if not directly, for the sad events in March and June, and because I am advancing in age, I would like to request party members to allow me to relinquish the duty of party chairman and as party member.

Initially people were unsure what this meant, but then his official resignation speech left little doubt that his legacy and influence would continue: "I want the entire nation, the people, to know that if in the future there are mob disturbances, if the army shoots, it hits. There will be no firing in the air to scare."

A few days later the nation had a better idea of what was in store when Ne Win tapped his successor: Brigadier-General Sein Lwin, the infamous "Butcher of Rangoon" who had commanded the White Bridge, Red Bridge massacre. Most Burmese people feared Sein Lwin as much as, if not more than, Ne Win. And though Ne Win gave up his title, he did not follow through on his promise to depart from public life. He retained his party membership and transferred power to a man who was a replicate of himself, if not his puppet.

THE 8.8.88 STRIKE

The second and more decisive event that galvanized Suu Kyi into action was a turning point for the entire nation. Within days of Sein Lwin's swearing in, posters and flyers encouraging a nationwide strike began circulating around Rangoon. A tentative date was set for August 8, or 8.8.88, just a few weeks away. Word of the strike spread to the rest of the country, partly due to the reporting of Christopher Gunness, a British journalist who was on hand to witness Ne Win's resignation and the transfer of power to Sein Lwin. Gunness's disclosure of the planned 8.8.88 strike diffused through the country's news agencies, and as early as August 1 students and monks from across Burma started descending on Rangoon in anticipation of a mass demonstration.

At precisely 8:08 a.m. on August 8, the capital's dock workers walked off the job, kicking off a general strike and a ripple of demonstrations across Burma. In Rangoon, hordes of people protested in front of city hall and other government buildings around the capital. The Tatmadaw and Lon Htein merely looked on as people chanted and marched, and for most of the day it appeared that Sein Lwin would not lash out. Students marched peacefully, demanding free and fair elections and a democratic, civilian-led government. They knelt down in front of the soldiers, singing to them of love and freedom and even pleading with them to come join their side.

Just before six o'clock that evening the crowd at city hall was warned to go home; otherwise they would be shot. For several hours nothing happened, but then, just before midnight, tanks

Burmese soldiers confronting demonstrators at a pro-democracy
rally in 1988 Rangoon

and army vehicles wheeled onto the streets and began firing at will. Army troops stationed outside the city were called in to mow down protesters. That night innocent civilians in Rangoon and in other cities across Burma were slaughtered, and the massacre continued for the next two days. Those not shot were imprisoned, many of them disappearing and never seen again. Protests and killing continued until August 12, when Sein Lwin announced his resignation. The army was ordered back to its garrisons and martial law was lifted.

Some 3,000 civilians in Rangoon alone were killed in what became known as the "Massacre of 8.8.88," and many more were killed outside the capital. The nature and scale of this indiscriminate killing eclipsed all other violence in Burma to date. The United States Senate and other governments the world over denounced Sein Lwin's actions and pledged their support for the democracy movement.

On August 19 Maung Maung, the attorney general of Burma, assumed the presidency. He had been the only civilian in Ne Win's regime, and this seemed to indicate at least a minor victory for the people's movement. Like Ne Win before him, he promised to hold a referendum on democracy, to let Burmese voters determine their fate. Rangoon's streets were already filled with people celebrating, but they wanted more than a referendum—they wanted democracy, right away.

STEPPING FORWARD

On August 15 Suu Kyi issued a letter to the Council of State of Burma, imploring the government to choose the good of the nation, not the good of the party. She also begged the government to release political prisoners and demonstrators.

The council ignored her letter. Protests erupted again, this time on a widespread scale, with demonstrations occurring in even the smallest villages around Burma. An estimated 50,000 people turned out on August 24 for a rally at Rangoon General Hospital. Writer and former newspaper editor Win Khet led the ceremonies, delivering a speech and conducting the crowd in spontaneous chants, such as "The people's nurses are our nurses," for two nurses who had pushed through the crowd on their way to work.

The greatest thunder of chanting and cheering came when Suu Kyi stepped up to the stage. Prior to then she had not participated in any of the protests, instead observing what was happening from inside her home. This was her first public appearance and it signaled her intention to take up the people's cause as her own, to play an active role in the democracy movement. Her address was short, but to the point: in two days she would deliver a speech at a rally at Rangoon's Shwedagon Pagoda. Agents of the government's intelligence unit were on hand at the hospital rally, and for the next two days the military regime did everything in its power to foil the Shwedagon speech. It spread word that Suu Kyi was not speaking at the Shwedagon, but at another location in the city. It also embarked on a slanderous propaganda campaign, distributing pamphlets that defamed Suu Kyi's character and claimed she was actually conspiring with a foreign country to take over Burma. Other leaflets condemned Aris as a communist Jew working for Moscow. Bomb scares and threats of assassination were spread in hopes that Suu Kyi would back down from speaking. Aris feared for his wife's safety as well as that of their sons.

On the morning of August 26 Suu Kyi left No. 54 with a convoy of vehicles guided by an old army jeep. Against the wish of her advisers she chose not to wear a bulletproof vest, though she did consent to a security detail of eight or nine unarmed young men. The caravan had to stop well short of the Shwedagon because the throng of people was so large. The crowd waved tricolor flags in homage to the French Revolution, and the brilliant robes of monks added to the festive mood. People had started to gather two days earlier, and approximately 1 million supporters showed up—an amazing turnout in a country with a population of 40 million.

As students and monks helped clear Suu Kyi's way to the stage, the crowd erupted into cheers. She addressed the rally from behind a small podium. Behind her diminutive figure was a

Suu Kyi speaks to her countrymen, hoping to inspire them
to pursue freedom.

huge portrait of her father, and in the eyes of the people, the father of free, independent Burma. Standing before his image and behind his cause for democracy, Suu Kyi began by remembering the students who had been killed in protests over the previous months. "It is the students who have paved the way. I therefore request you all to observe a minute's silence . . . for those students who have lost their lives."

THE DUTIFUL DAUGHTER

After the pause for remembrance, Suu Kyi explained her decision to join the movement. Some Burmese were skeptical, even critical, of her commitment because she had not lived in Burma since she was a teenager. Suu Kyi defended against these claims, "It is true that I have lived abroad [and] am married to a foreigner. These facts have never interfered and will never interfere with or lessen my love and devotion for my country." Some critics went so far as calling her opportunistic, arguing that she had no real connection to or understanding of Burma's struggle; she was simply exploiting her present circumstance, which she had entered only because her mother fell ill. Suu Kyi rebutted this allegation in her speech as well:

> Some people have been saying [that] I know nothing of Burmese politics. The trouble is that I know too much. My family knows best how complicated and tricky Burmese politics can be and how much my father had to suffer on this account.

Like her father, Suu Kyi had always been disinclined to enter politics. Aung San's desire had been to achieve Burma's independence, but not to take part in politics after independence was won. "Since my father had no such desire," Suu Kyi assured the crowd at the Shwedagon,

> I too have always wanted to place myself at a distance from . . . politics. Some might then ask why . . . should I now be involved in this movement. The answer is that . . . I could not as my father's daughter remain indifferent to all that [is] going on.

She described the situation in Burma as a "national crisis" and declared it the "second struggle for national independence."

Aung San had struggled for independence from foreign colonial powers more than forty years earlier; Suu Kyi now found herself facing Burma's own despotic leaders. For direction in this "second struggle," Suu Kyi invoked her father's wisdom, citing a quote of his:

> We must make democracy the popular creed. We must try to build up a free Burma in accordance with such a creed. If we should fail to do this, our people are bound to suffer. . . . Democracy is the only ideology which is consistent with freedom. It is also the only ideology that promotes and strengthens peace. It is therefore the only ideology we should aim for.

She implored leaders of the various opposition groups to put aside their differences and join together under the cause of national unity, an appeal that would become the refrain of her democracy campaign. A united country, Suu believed, would best be able to achieve peace and democracy.

The Bogyoke's daughter also challenged the nation to forgive the ruling army and the police for the bloody events of the previous months, excessive and cruel though they were. The army must, in her words, "become a force in which the people can place their trust and reliance. May the armed forces become one which will uphold the honor and dignity of our country." And finally, she warned against simply trying to remove certain individuals from the one-party government. Promises of reform and referendum delivered by the government were shallow; anything short of a multi-party system with free and fair elections was an unacceptable compromise.

Seventeen years later, under voluntary exile in Thailand, U Win Khet looked back on the rally at the Shwedagon Pagoda:

> What surprised me, what surprised us all, was how mature she was. She spoke elegantly but simply, so that everyone could understand exactly what she meant. It may be an old man's delusion, but for me she became Aung San in August 1988. Her actions, her commitment, most of all her manner, were exactly like his.

Shwedagon Pagoda

Burma was once one of Southeast Asia's richest countries, but decades of misrule by the country's military dictatorship have left it one of the poorest. Many ordinary Burmese find it difficult to feed their families, and vendors like the women and girl pictured here earn the little they do by selling fruits and vegetables at open markets.

THE DEMOCRACY
MOVEMENT TAKES SHAPE

A few days after the Shwedagon speech, journalist Karan Thapar interviewed Suu Kyi for the *Times of London*. She asked Suu to comment on the role she might play in the democratic government; Suu reiterated that her intention was to "be of most use in bringing about a peaceful transition," but that "a life in politics holds no attraction for me." She considered herself a "unifying force" because of her father's legacy, but she had no interest in "jostling for any kind of position."

Despite her reluctance to enter politics, Suu Kyi undeniably was one of the main leaders of the democracy movement; the others were Aung Gyi, U Tin Oo, and U Nu. U Nu had recently formed the League for Democracy and Peace, an alliance that Suu, and eventually the other two men, joined. Although Aung Gyi and U Tin Oo were committed to the democracy movement, John Parenteau points out that their past was slightly tainted— initially they had served in Ne Win's administration before losing his approval. On the other hand, U Nu had been prime minister after Suu Kyi's father was assassinated, and though his "democratic credentials were second only to Aung San himself," he was eighty-one years old. Younger and less experienced than the other three men as she was, Suu Kyi's speech at the Shwedagon had affirmed her popularity, and it gradually fell to her to take charge. No. 54 became the League's unofficial headquarters, and it was there that she, Aung Gyi, Tin Oo, and U Nu started directing the democracy movement's agenda.

Toward the end of August convicted criminals started "escaping" from prisons around Burma. The League for Democracy and Peace joined other opposition leaders in blaming the government for releasing prisoners on purpose, maintaining that the military regime had done so to trigger even more chaos on Burma's streets. Whether the prisoners escaped or were freed, the result was pandemonium. Prior to Suu Kyi's address on August 26, protests and confrontations between protesters and the army—though violent—had been the extent of unrest. Now, with thousands of prisoners roaming free, a country already beset by political demonstrations and strikes was in danger of slipping into a state of emergency. Criminal activity spread rapidly, and it seemed the police were powerless or unwilling to control the looting and rioting. Many people anticipated another harsh crackdown by the military, if not an all-out civil war.

Amidst the lawlessness, some factions of the protest movement decided to take matters into their own hands. They accused some of their own members of being Lon Htein spies and put them to trial. The proceedings were but a sham; accused spies were sentenced to death and countless killings were carried out. If Suu Kyi heard news that such illegal mock trials were taking place, she and others would rush to prevent the executions, pleading that the cruelty stop. In the face of increased violence and now lawlessness, some opposition leaders considered Suu Kyi's message of peaceful resistance inadequate.

Demonstrations in front of the United States Embassy typically were safer than most; protesters assumed the military police would not do anything to provoke the United States government. However, a rally in front of the embassy in late August threatened to get out of hand. Soldiers confronted the protesters and threatened to shoot and kill unless the crowd disbanded and went home. Unfazed by the threat, a bold young teenager stepped forward from the crowd and ripped open his shirt. He paused and held his arms out wide, offering his bare chest as a target for the soldiers to shoot. There was reason to believe that the army might fire on the young boy, as they had done before, but on this day the soldiers refrained. They put down their weapons and allowed the peaceful rally to continue.

In the first week of September, Maung Maung, now Burma's minister of health, lifted martial law. He released from prison the military officers that had opposed Ne Win, including Aung Gyi, and the newly formed Bar Council declared that Ne Win's 1962 military coup had been illegal. Trade and professional unions reformed and claimed rights that the junta had denied them, and several leaders came forward to fill the power vacuum created by revoking martial law. A power struggle ensued, and clashes between these groups drowned out Suu Kyi's plea for unity.

The United States sought to help with Burma's transition to civilian law. It sent Congressman Stephen Solarz to Rangoon to broker an agreement between Maung Maung's administration and the senior leaders of the democracy movement. No deal was reached, and Congressman Solarz returned home to urge the U.S. Congress to stop supporting the Burmese government's counter-narcotics program. U.S. aid was best diverted away from the corrupt government and toward the democracy movement.

On September 9, U Nu surprised the nation by declaring himself Burma's rightful leader because he had been prime minister when Ne Win seized power illegally in 1962. His announcement confused supporters of the opposition and raised doubts about whether the League for Democracy and Peace was capable of achieving its goals. The BBC (British Broadcasting Corporation) interviewed U Nu the following day and asked whether he

Congressman Stephen Solarz
in 1989

99

had consulted with Suu Kyi and other leaders before claiming his right to the presidency. To the detriment of the already struggling democracy movement he replied, "Why do you think that we need to consult with them? You give me the answer. . . . They can do what they want, I will not object and I will do what I want."

Aung Gyi and Suu Kyi jumped to distance themselves from U Nu, but as it turned out his initiative was quick to collapse. U Tin Oo originally had considered joining U Nu, but he quickly pulled out and sided with Suu Kyi and Aung Gyi.

Four days before U Nu's surprise announcement, Congressman Solarz had stopped in Bangkok on his way home. At a press conference there he reported that his talks had not generated consensus between the Burmese government and opposition leaders. He also warned that a "devastating civil war" would follow if the ruling military did not agree to reform. Over the next week, foreign governments began evacuating diplomats and their families from embassies. The situation in Burma was becoming dire.

U Nu, left, Aung San Suu Kyi, center, and General Tin Oo

A REVOLUTION OF THE SPIRIT

Reforms were made in September 1988, but as with the previous transfer of power, the people had not been given a say and the new government would prove even more repressive and brutal than before. Already in August there was speculation that Ne Win had convened a secret council at his home on Inya Lake, with the goal of devising a plan to crush the democracy movement. It was uncertain how organized the council was, but when the announcement came on September 18 that Maung Maung had been removed from office and replaced by General Saw Maung, another military crackdown seemed imminent.

The previous day, hundreds of pro-democracy protesters had gathered outside of the Ministry of Trade in Rangoon. They incited the building's security guards to fire their guns, killing one of the protesters. This time, the mob of demonstrators retaliated by swarming the Ministry and taking some twenty soldiers hostage. After being disarmed, the soldiers were transferred to monks at a local monastery. This had been the last straw for Ne Win. He tapped General Saw Maung as chief of state and commander of a military junta that would reign for the next nine years.

General Maung sat atop the State Law and Order Restoration Council, or SLORC, a governing body of nineteen members, mostly senior military officers. The Tatmadaw would become the Council's primary agent for "restoring order," and it acted swiftly. By the morning of September 21 the uprising was defeated. In a matter of less than four days, military troops across all of Burma had stormed the streets of villages and cities alike, killing dissidents and ordering people to stay at home. Most victims were killed during open fire on the streets, but some were systematically executed en masse—one group gathered outside Rangoon city hall was rounded up and thrown into fire pits.

Before he was deposed, Maung Maung had promised the democracy movement he would hold multiparty elections. Surprisingly, the SLORC announced it would carry out that promise and go forward with "free and fair elections"—sometime in the future. As a start, the SLORC authorized political parties to form. By the end of 1989 more than 230 parties would register with the state. Among these was the National League for Democracy, registered in October 1988 with Suu Kyi as its leader.

The SLORC takeover had pushed Suu Kyi over the edge. She could have shrugged her shoulders, surrendered all hope, and returned to England. Peaceful Oxford and her family awaited her, as did her budding academic career. Many people inside and outside Burma had already lost hope. British ambassador Martin Morland reckoned "a free-for-all election campaign after the present clampdown looks as likely as a happy ending to Macbeth." But the daughter of Aung San would not back down. In anticipation of the elections, she and other NLD leaders feverishly began organizing their party and establishing a base of support across the country.

Between August 1988 and July 1989, Suu Kyi gave nearly a thousand speeches in her "Revolution of the Spirit" campaign. Suu Kyi also took her cause to the world. For years her position had been that change in Burma must come from within, but she also recognized the valuable role foreign governments and international organizations could play in applying pressure on the military regime. She wrote several letters to Amnesty International pleading for it to intervene and to persuade other international organizations to provide assistance. She also issued an open letter to foreign ministers attending the United Nations Assembly, urging them to condemn the SLORC's "indiscriminate killing . . . of unarmed demonstrators including school children, students and Buddhist monks." It took some time, but in the end international pressuring, mostly expressed through sanctions and embargoes, helped erode the SLORC's power base.

In the remaining months of 1988 the NLD experienced progress, but not without intermittent setbacks, including a dispute with party leader Aung Gyi that led to his ousting. He had been an early ally of Suu Kyi and U Tin Oo, but his reputation as a trustworthy leader had been questionable, as he remained chummy with members of the SLORC. Ultimately his exit benefited the NLD, as Suu Kyi emerged as the frontrunner of the party.

Suu Kyi addresses a rally in Rangoon in 1989.

As Suu Kyi's popularity increased, Ne Win and the SLORC unleashed a propaganda campaign aimed at vilifying her. Its accusations were based on two main allegations. Firstly, her marriage to a foreigner and decades-long exile from Burma proved she was anything but a patriot. How could she embrace and marry into the culture that her father had spent his life battling against? The SLORC depicted her as an outsider, having returned to Burma and remained there adventitiously, exploiting its volatile political situation for her own personal gain.

The SLORC's second line of attack involved labeling Suu Kyi and the NLD as a communist conspiracy. The Communist Party of Burma had been waging civil war against the military and other insurgent groups since 1940. It had a poor reputation, and many Burmese were hostile toward it for fomenting trouble in whatever regions it entered. When the democracy movement formed, the NLD had welcomed some reformed communists into its fold; the SLORC spun this to suggest Suu Kyi and the NLD were extremists. It spread these and other rumors about Suu Kyi, even distributing posters with obscene drawings of her.

With the government censoring the national media, Suu Kyi and the NLD had little recourse to challenge the SLORC's accusations—even though the NLD was granted legal status, it was effectively banned from publicizing itself in print. Suu Kyi and the other leaders sidestepped this obstacle with the help of foreign journalists, who reported on their behalf to the British Broadcasting Corporation (BBC) and the Voice of America by shortwave radio. For those Burmese not around to witness in Rangoon, illegal video footage of Suu Kyi's speeches became extremely sought after, in some cases more than videos of popular American rock groups (which were also outlawed). There are reports of some people paying a week's wages for black-market videos of Suu Kyi speaking about democracy.

CRUEL PUNISHMENT

Daw Khin Kyi passed away at her home on December 27, 1988. Her funeral on January 2, 1989, marked a turning point for the NLD. More than 100,000 people turned out to line the streets of Rangoon for her funeral procession, many of them waving the NLD flag. The SLORC refrained from cracking down—after all, people were mourning the loss of the wife of Aung San. Even the SLORC and Ne Win laid claim to the Bogyoke, but that so many people turned out to pay their respects, and that the day's events proceeded peacefully, concerned them. The procession was not intended as a political rally, but those who came out to honor Daw Khin Kyi—certainly those displaying NLD colors— had also come to show Suu Kyi that they stood behind her. And standing behind Suu Kyi meant standing opposite the SLORC.

After announcing that a general election would be held in the spring of 1990, the SLORC stepped up its harassment of anyone lending support to the democracy movement. Now, instead of opening fire on Burma's streets, it acted more covertly. Suu Kyi began campaigning around the country, and SLORC operatives monitored who attended her speeches. They apprehended the most loyal and able NLD supporters, usually students, and either imprisoned them or forced them to serve in ongoing wars against insurgent forces. While waiting to be shipped off to battlefronts, many students were subject to cruel forms of punishment, such as being stripped naked and herded around like animals. Others were brought to mine fields and forced to walk across them as human minesweepers.

Troops arresting a student at a National League
for Democracy (NLD) rally

As spring warmed to summer, another momentous and potentially riotous day drew closer. July 19 was Martyrs' Day, commemorating Aung San's death. The nation had paid homage to the Bogyoke on that date every year since his assassination, and 1989 would be no exception. Suu Kyi and the other leaders of the NLD took charge in organizing the commemoration program, which included a march from her home on University Avenue to the Shwedagon. In the weeks prior to July 19 Suu made several public addresses in Rangoon that drew massive crowds—the largest was one at the Sule Pagoda, with an estimated 30,000 people on hand.

For the SLORC to prohibit people from honoring the Bogyoke would only further enrage the antigovernment movement. Ne Win's fear, however, was that Martyrs' Day might turn into a massive political demonstration. To prevent that from happening, the SLORC announced that individual acts of tribute were permissible, but marches, rallies, and any gathering of five or more people was illegal. On the evening of July 18, thousands of Tatmadaw soldiers, bearing automatic weapons and fixed bayonets, filled Rangoon's streets. They laid barbed wire across the main streets and drove trucks throughout the townships, announcing a special daytime curfew would be in place from 6:00 a.m. to 6:00 p.m. for July 19th.

Fearing arrests and renewed violence, at the last moment Suu Kyi called a halt to all plans for Martyrs' Day. She would privately honor her father's memory on the following day instead. Her sons, seventeen-year-old Alexander and twelve-year-old Kim, had arrived the week before and would join her in honoring their grandfather. Aris had planned to come with them, but his own father's death kept him with his family in Scotland.

July 19 came and went. Then, on the morning of the 20th, Suu Kyi awoke to sounds of clanking, hammering, and other noises coming from outside her house. Teams of soldiers were stringing barbed wire across the roads leading to her home; others stood guard around the perimeter of the property and prevented anyone from entering or exiting. No. 54 was under siege by the military.

Suu Kyi worked at keeping everyone calm. Breakfast would be served as usual. She tried calling Aris in Scotland, to no avail—Burma's international telephone lines had been cut off. When she tried to leave and take flowers to her father's grave, as she had planned, soldiers turned her back at gunpoint. Later that afternoon government officials knocked at her door and informed her she was under house arrest. Only a maid and a cook were allowed to remain with her and her sons.

Suu Kyi gathered together the forty students and other NLD leaders who had been staying at the compound with her. She instructed them to leave at once and not to resist arrest—there

Armed Burmese soldiers are on the lookout from a guardhouse built near Aung San Suu Kyi's residence in Rangoon.

were soldiers waiting outside with orders to apprehend them. All of Suu Kyi's advisers and organizers were carted away to jail, where they received prison sentences ranging from a few months to several years. All across Rangoon the SLORC had ordered similar arrests.

Once under house arrest, the government gave Suu Kyi the option of leaving Burma, with the caveat that she would never be allowed to return. Without Suu Kyi leading the opposition, went the SLORC's logic, the movement for democracy would wither to nothing and the military would retain absolute power. But the SLORC had miscalculated—Suu Kyi was not about to leave her country now. She even asked to receive the same treatment as the other political prisoners, but Ne Win knew better. If anything happened to her, it would be to his detriment and to the benefit of the NLD.

Suu Kyi began a hunger strike after she was placed under house arrest, demanding that other arrested NLD supporters be treated humanely. She refused to take any food, only liquids—water and fruit juices. Her health declined in the subsequent weeks, and only after the government promised not to subject its political prisoners to cruel treatment did she end her fast. Doctors rushed to see her and applied an intravenous drip to rejuvenate her feeble body.

Taking Up Her Father's Mission

Around this time Aris left Scotland for Rangoon to be with his family. He and Suu Kyi did not want Kim and Alexander to witness their mother's decline; he also wanted to encourage and comfort Suu Kyi in her struggle against her oppressors. The SLORC feared that Aris would liaise with what remained of the NLD leadership on behalf of his wife, and as soon as his plane touched down in Rangoon, soldiers escorted him to a private detention room. Government officials informed him that he would be allowed to spend two weeks with his wife and sons, but he would be deported immediately if he made contact with anyone outside their home.

From then until he left, the outside world had no knowledge of Aris's situation or whereabouts. "For twenty-two days I effectively disappeared from sight. Nobody knew what had happened to me," he recalled. Despite being under the unnerving watch of Tatmadaw soldiers at No. 54, Aris, Suu Kyi, and their sons spent glorious days with each other.

Aris and the boys were permitted to extend their visit into September, but then it was time for Alexander and Kim to return to school in England. Before leaving Rangoon, Aris met with the SLORC and requested that Suu Kyi be allowed to receive letters and packages from him; he wished to send her books and personal belongings from their home in Oxford. The SLORC granted his request, but not without an expense to the family. After Aris and the boys arrived back in England, Burma's embassy in London informed Aris that the Burmese passports belonging to Alexander and Kim had been revoked. The boys were stripped of their citizenship and forbidden from reentering Burma, not even with a visa on their British passports.

The SLORC was forcing Suu Kyi to choose between her family and her homeland. Aris later observed that, "very obviously the [SLORC's] plan was to break Suu Kyi's spirit by separating her from her children in the hope she would accept permanent exile." Unless she left Burma, Suu Kyi had seen her sons for the last time. And if she did leave, she would never be allowed to return.

This was bleak news. Aris had known that the time might come when his wife would take up her father's mission as her own, and that this might impose hardship on their family, but he was committed to supporting her. Fortunately he was not prevented from returning to Burma, and that Christmas he flew back to be with Suu Kyi.

He arrived bearing a suitcase full of presents for Suu Kyi, and each day he gave her one to open. Near the end of their two weeks together Suu Kyi thought she had opened them all, but Aris surprised her with one last special gift. An Oxford colleague of his, law professor John Finnis, had forwarded her name to the

Suu Kyi and Aris at her home during her house arrest

Nobel Committee, requesting she be considered for the Nobel Peace Prize. Receiving the Nobel Prize would be a tremendous personal accomplishment for Suu Kyi, but it could also help bolster the movement for democracy and human rights in Burma. With Suu Kyi in extreme isolation and the SLORC having cordoned off the country from the outside world, Burma stood to profit from any support that the international community might extend.

Aris's visit provided Suu Kyi with much needed companionship and inspiration, and he later wrote that "the days I spent alone with her . . . completely isolated from the world, are among my happiest memories of our many years of marriage." He suspected that he had been allowed to visit her because "the authorities had hoped I would try to persuade her to leave with me. In fact, knowing the strength of Suu's determination, I had not even thought of doing this." The SLORC had misjudged Suu Kyi, and for that matter Aris. Its hard line had strengthened her resolve. and she would stay the course in Burma, even if it meant life under house arrest.

The guardhouse at Suu Kyi's residence was used to monitor No. 54
University Avenue during her house arrest.

Many children in Burma live desperate lives. Approximately one in ten dies before reaching age five from preventable or treatable diseases such as malaria (the number one killer), diarrhea, pneumonia, and tuberculosis. One in three under the age of five is malnourished. Children are vulnerable in other ways, too. For more than twenty years, Burma's Armed Forces has recruited and used child soldiers as young as nine, and according to human trafficking experts, children from Burma are regularly trafficked to neighboring China, Thailand, India, and Bangladesh for sexual exploitation, domestic servitude, and forced labor. To protect their children, as well as ensure that they are well fed, educated, and enjoy permanent shelter, parents of children as young as five allow them to become novices in the hundreds of monasteries and nunneries in this deeply religious Buddhist country.

chapter eight

POLITICAL PRISONER
AND LAUREATE

S hortly after Aris left Burma, the SLORC effectively outlawed any expression of support for Suu Kyi. It became a crime to wear an Aung San Suu Kyi t-shirt or badge, even to possess a picture of her. Government officers erected large signs outside her home, warning drivers "Do Not Slow Down" and "No U Turns." But these and other attempts to keep the democracy movement in check were counterproductive. Suu Kyi's house arrest actually propelled the NLD forward; it gained more momentum every day she remained locked up, even when the SLORC ruled in early 1990 that she would not be able to stand for election.

Suu Kyi refused to accept food from the SLORC. She sold most of the furniture and some amenities in the crumbling white villa that had been her mother's house in order to buy her own food. She also maintained a strict routine "to avoid a feckless squandering of time."

Each day she rose before five in the morning and began her routine of meditation and exercise. She followed national news on the radio—if she was granted access. She also played piano for hours at a time, and many Rangoon residents would sneak up to the house just to hear her play. When word spread that her piano was broken, people assumed that it stopped working properly because of overuse, but she later admitted to a rare moment of rage—pounding the piano after learning that a dear friend had been tortured. The piano manufacturer Steinway contacted U.S.

officials in Washington with an offer to repair her piano, but the SLORC did not entertain such negotiations.

Because her telephone did not always work, Suu Kyi could not count on being able to make or receive calls. Nor could she count on receiving mail or visitors. In a published "Letter from Burma," she wrote:

> In Burma, one should approach the telephone with a prayer on the lips and a determination to try, try and try again. Getting through to the required number at the first attempt is such an event to greet with incredulity and an expression of thanks to all powers, seen and unseen. The post office is no more reliable then the telephone system. I cannot quite make up my mind whether so many letters addressed to me fail to arrive because of the inefficiency of the post office or because of the efficiency of the Military Intelligence. My dear Japanese teacher Michiko-san sent me a little note through somebody who came to Rangoon to let me know she has been writing to me regularly through the post. None of those letters have reached me. Other friends also send messages to tell me they have written but their letters have not arrived either. Lately, the authorities have even prohibited courier services from delivering magazines and papers addressed to me.

With plenty of time to contemplate and reflect, Suu Kyi found solace in a large batik portrait of her father, hanging on a wall in the living room. It is the same poster Suu Kyi used at her first public speech at Shwedagon Pagoda in 1988. "I think of him as nice and human, not as a cold, marble hero. Sometimes I think to myself, 'Just you and me, isn't it?'"

Suu Kyi poses in front of a portrait of her father at her home in 1995.

Popular elections took place in Burma on May 27, 1990, the first since 1960. The government authorized multiple political parties to participate and promised the elections would be free and fair. It even permitted Western journalists to travel to Burma and witness the voting, presumably in the hope that they would report to the world that the proceedings were legitimate. The night before, the nationwide curfew was lifted, and on election day members of the Tatmadaw and other law enforcement agencies were scarcely seen on the streets. Still, there was reason to believe these measures were but a ruse. Suu Kyi was under house arrest, and she and other NLD candidates, including U Tin Oo, had been disqualified from the election.

The government planned to wait until June 14 to announce the official outcome, but for some reason it allowed individual districts to publicize results as soon as ballots were counted. The earliest count came from a township in Rangoon, where Daw San San, an NLD candidate, had defeated her opponents by a wide margin. This was the first in a massive wave of victories for the NLD. After all the ballots were tallied, the NLD had won almost two-thirds of the popular vote and more than 80 percent of seats to the legislature.

The SLORC had lost in a landslide to Suu Kyi's party. In a desperate, last-ditch effort to preserve its mandate, it contrived to change the rules. Authorities declared that votes had not been cast to elect a new government, but only to elect delegates to a constituent assembly. That body would then debate whether and how a new constitution might be written. Moreover, the assembly would not convene until the framework of a new constitution was in place. The SLORC was responsible for laying this framework, which it actually had no intention of doing. The elections had come to naught, and worse still, Suu Kyi's house arrest—originally meant to last only until after the elections—was extended for another year.

The number and brutality of protests and arrests increased after the fraudulent elections, and violence was still on the rise when the anniversary of 8.8.88 rolled around. Buddhist monks once again broke their vows against political activity and led a rally in Mandalay, the country's second-largest city, located in central Burma. The human rights group Asian Watch later issued a report stating that "torture, including electric shocks, beatings, sleep deprivation and cigarette burns" was widespread across Burma. By the end of 1990 any public expression advocating democracy was forbidden. Suu Kyi's cousin, Sein Win, was one of the last NLD leaders not yet in prison. He escaped the country to Thailand, where he proclaimed a rival government-in-exile.

Nations around the world condemned the Burmese government for abusing its citizens and tampering with the political process. Many of them stopped aiding Burma altogether, as their contributions mostly ended up in the coffers of SLORC chiefs and never trickled down to the people. In order to maintain control and finance its military, the government was forced to sell most of Burma's assets, including rights and access to the country's natural resources. It allowed companies from Thailand to raze forests to the ground, and it sold large holdings of oil fields to Western corporations. This perpetuated the SLORC's wealth, but profits were not distributed back into the Burmese economy. One of the most tragic effects of the government's greed was

Burmese children sawing a log

an increase in infant mortality rates. In her book *Letters from Burma*, Suu Kyi attributed this trend to "malnutrition, lack of access to safe water and sanitation, lack of access to health services and lack of caring capacity, which includes programmes for childhood development, primary education and health education."

Human rights groups and other international organizations joined foreign governments in turning up the pressure on Burma, and word of Suu Kyi's story began to spread. Norway awarded her its Thorolf Rafto Prize for Human Rights, and in July 1991 she received the European Parliament's Sakharov Prize for Freedom of Thought, named for the Russian physicist and political dissident Andrei Sakharov. Then a momentous announcement came on October 14, 1991: the Norwegian Nobel Committee would award its Nobel Peace Prize to Aung San Suu Kyi.

Still under house arrest, Suu Kyi was prevented from attending the award presentation in Oslo, Norway. In his remarks at the ceremony, Professor Francis Sejersted, chairman of the Nobel committee, praised Suu Kyi for "bring[ing] out something of the best in us. We feel we need precisely her sort of person in order to retain our faith in the future. That is what gives her such power as a symbol, and that is why any ill-treatment feels like a violation of what we have most at heart."

After Sejersted's laudation, young Alexander Aris stepped to the podium on stage and accepted the award on behalf of his mother. Flanked by his father and brother, he read from a speech his father helped him prepare:

> I know that she would begin by saying that she accepts the Nobel Prize not in her own name but in the name of all the people of Burma. . . . [If] she were free today my mother would . . . ask you to pray that the oppressors and the oppressed would throw down their weapons and join together to build a nation founded on humanity in the spirit of peace.

Alexander Aris, center, Suu Kyi's older son, accepts the Nobel Peace Prize "in the name of all the people of Burma" from the head of the Norwegian Nobel Peace Prize Committee, Francis Sejersted, left, at the award ceremony in Oslo, Norway, on December 10, 1991. On the right is Suu Kyi's younger son Kim.

The prize came with an award in the amount of roughly $1.2 million, which Suu Kyi invested toward promoting better health and education in Burma.

A Bittersweet Family Reunion

When Suu Kyi won the Nobel Prize, Michael Aris released a statement to the press. He believed that such a distinction could bolster the democracy movement in Burma. It could also help energize similar uprisings around the world. "Many will now for the first time learn of her courageous leadership of the non-violent struggle for . . . human rights in her country. I believe her role will come to serve as an inspiration to a great number of people in the world today."

But Aris's tone shifted from hopeful to somber when reflecting on Suu Kyi's situation and their family's separation. Suu was in her third year of confinement and had not seen her husband and sons for two years:

> We, her family, are denied any contact whatsoever with her and know nothing of her condition except that she is quite alone. We do not even know if she is still kept in her own house or if she has been moved elsewhere. . . . I hope our family's situation will be eased as a result of this supreme gesture of recognition . . . and that we may at last be allowed to pay her visits again.

Under Burmese law, a person considered a threat to state security can be arrested and detained without trial for three years. Until they are tried, prisoners are denied visits from family members. Suu Kyi fell into this category, but unlike other detainees, at least she could rest assured that her family was safe and financially secure in England. Her fellow political prisoners did not have that same peace of mind, as their families were at risk living in Burma.

In late April the Burmese Embassy in England summoned Aris to its London office. Officials there had called him in a month earlier requesting that he write Suu Kyi and urge her to leave Burma. He refused, knowing full well that she would not go along with it. On arriving at the embassy the second time around in April, he was surprised to learn that the Burmese government had reversed its position and also lifted his travel ban. He made plans to fly to Rangoon directly and arrived there on May 2.

At long last the couple was reunited, but Aris could only stay for two weeks. He stopped in Bangkok on his way home to address the international press corps there. His remarks were short and somewhat vague, given the sensitivity of Suu Kyi's situation. He reported that she remained upbeat and in good health, but that she would not be leaving Burma.

To Suu Kyi's joy, the Burmese government also cleared her sons to reenter Burma with their British passports. They came separately after their father and spent a week at No. 54. Two years without seeing one's family is a long time, and Suu Kyi described her reaction at seeing Kim as being similar to stories she heard of other prisoners:

> A political prisoner failed to recognize the teenager who came to see him on his first family visit after more than two years in detention as the young son he had left behind. It was a situation that was familiar to me. When I saw my younger son again for the first time after a separation of two years and seven months he had changed from a round faced not-quite-twelve-year-old into a rather stylish "cool" teenager. If I had met him in the street I would not have known him for my little son.

Michael Aris with his sons, Kim, center, and Alexander, at Heathrow Airport in London

BURMA VERSUS FAMILY

Suu Kyi remained under house arrest, but compared to the tumultuous period of 1988–1989, political tensions in Burma had subsided considerably. In an attempt to lure foreign investors and increase trade, the ruling junta touted economic and political reform. It also promoted Burma as a welcome destination for international tourists, and the campaign seemed to be working. Not only was Suu Kyi's family allowed to come to Burma, but some brave visitors from Asia and other parts of the world started showing up on their vacations. The SLORC even permitted *New York Times* journalist Philip Shenon and U.S. congressman Bill Richardson to pay Suu a visit at No. 54—though they were chaperoned by an official and their conversations were recorded.

For the next couple of years nothing really changed in Burma. Then, in the last quarter of 1994, after many months without a visitor, Suu Kyi was taken to meet General Than Shwe, who had replaced Saw Maung as head of state in 1992, and Khin Nyunt, Burma's chief of military intelligence. What was said in their conversation was never disclosed, but their meeting seemed to indicate the SLORC might be loosening its grip over Suu Kyi and willing to involve the NLD in the political process.

Regardless of what their discussion concerned, this meeting proved a good omen. On July 10, 1995, the government did more than ease restrictions on Suu Kyi or invite her to meet SLORC officials—it released her from house arrest. That afternoon, just days shy of six years since she had been detained, Rangoon's chief of police pulled up to her home and told her she was free. The government never came forward with a specific reason for letting her go, but several factors seem to have influenced its decision. The military had made headway against several insurgent groups; there was the prospect of international financial support if the state opened up its political process to include other parties; and the NLD seemed to have lost its vitality in Suu Kyi's six-year absence.

Once again, the SLORC had underestimated Aung San Suu Kyi. Within hours, those former advisers of hers who were not in prison, including U Tin Oo, returned to No. 54 and began right where they had left off six years before. Loyal supporters began gathering outside of her home as well, and by morning on the next day thousands of people had flocked to University Avenue to celebrate her release. After meeting with U Tin Oo and others, Suu Kyi came to the gate at the entrance to her property and delivered a rousing speech, welcomed with loud bursts of applause and cheering. This was the first of many weekly addresses, dubbed "gateside chats," that she made from outside her home. Beginning each Friday afternoon, the streets around

Suu Kyi stands behind her gate to greet a crowd of an estimated 1,000 people who have come to see her on July 11, 1995, after her release from house arrest.

No. 54 filled with people waiting on Suu Kyi to appear before them and speak, and an air of festive revelry suffused University Avenue until sundown on Sundays.

During the week she and the NLD leadership worked around the clock to attend to the party's business. As in 1988 and 1989, No. 54 became a hive of activity, and before long there was a steady stream of visitors coming to meet her and pay their respects. In addition to her Burmese supporters, a great many international activists, journalists, and diplomats also arrived to consult with and interview her. One such visitor was Alan Clements, whom Suu agreed to sit with for a series of conversations that would later be published as a book, *The Voice of Hope*. Clements was well acquainted with Burma's cultural and political landscape. A convert to Buddhism, he had spent five years at the same monastery as U Tin Oo during the early 1980s. He went on to found the Burma Project, a nonprofit organization devoted to fighting human rights abuses in Burma.

Their conversations took place over several months between the winter of 1995 and the summer of 1996. She reflected on her imprisonment, her religious views, and her outlook on Burma's future. "Nothing has changed since my release," she told Clements. "Let the world know that we are still prisoners in our own country." From the government-in-exile in Thailand, Thaung Htun, a member of the national coalition government there, came to the same conclusion: "The human rights situation cannot be measured only by murders and tortures. It should be measured by fear. And by that standard, the entire population of 42 million people are imprisoned in Burma."

Madeleine Albright, the U.S. ambassador to the United Nations at the time, was also struck by the pervasive fear lurking in Burma.

> Khin Nyunt [head of military intelligence] expressed the belief that the SLORC had broad public support, and observed that the Burmese people smile a lot. I said that it has been my

experience, in a lifetime of studying repressive societies, that dictators often delude themselves into believing they have popular support, but that people often smile not because they are happy, but because they are afraid.

Now, in Suu Kyi, people found hope and vitality, a leader whom they could trust and who inspired courage, not fear. In their eyes she had emerged victorious, having survived the SLORC's heavy hand. When Clements asked her if the SLORC had ever assailed her emotionally or mentally, she replied, "No and I think this is because I have never learned to hate them . . . if I had really started hating my captors, hating the SLORC and the army, I would have defeated myself."

SPREADING THE MESSAGE

Upon being released from house arrest Suu Kyi quickly took advantage of her newfound freedom and mobility. Traveling by car across Burma, she met with supporters and spread her message of unity and democracy. She was usually welcomed wherever she went, but as the nation began rallying around her, the SLORC feared its control was threatened. It began a campaign of harassment against Suu Kyi and her followers. Unshaken by the SLORC's intimidation tactics, Suu Kyi plowed forward with her own campaign—even in November 1996, when a group of hostile opponents attacked her car. When asked about the incident in an interview, she explained her choice not to cancel the rally at which she was engaged to speak.

> I made the decision that we were simply going to continue on to meet the crowds that had come to support us. One of the boys who was in the car with us was a bit angry about the whole thing, so I spent some time calming him down and telling him not to be angry. But it was clear to us that the attack was a deliberate attempt to harm us badly or even kill us.

The SLORC kept arresting NLD members, and though this troubled Suu Kyi, it seemed also to strengthen her resolve. She attacked the government, and many international leaders came to her side. In 1996, U.S. President Bill Clinton supported a law passed in Congress that prohibited U.S. companies from investing any further in Burma; it also prohibited anyone belonging to SLORC (including family members) from obtaining visas to travel to the U.S. Such measures did little to intimidate the SLORC, nor did a harsh report issued by a special UN commission that same year.

Further efforts were made by the government to bully NLD supporters. Party offices were shut down in various parts of the country, and members were imprisoned or sentenced to years of hard labor, seemingly at random. The military police also set up a checkpoint outside Suu Kyi's home and screened all incoming visitors. It banned public gatherings and smothered peaceful rallies held on university campuses.

Twice in the summer of 1998 the Tatmadaw stopped Suu Kyi and her motorcade on the road. She demanded that the caravan be allowed to proceed, but the blockades held their ground. On the first occasion, after being trapped inside her car for five days, soldiers forcibly removed her and returned her to No. 54. On the second occasion, six days passed before she was made to turn around. In both cases, in response to public outcries, the government issued statements to the public claiming that they had contained Suu Kyi for her own safety. Since she had arrived in Rangoon in 1988, attempts to demoralize Suu Kyi—and in the process topple the NLD—had ranged from disqualifying her from national elections; to keeping her locked up in her own home; to making a mockery of her rights as a free woman, in one case even turning a blind eye to a mob of hoodlums that attacked her car with sticks and stones. Adding insult to injury, the junta had also kept her isolated from her family. Suu Kyi endured the years of punishment, isolation, and disrespect with dignity, never compromising her ideals in order to counter the government's malevolence. Many people wondered just how much more she was willing to endure, and some even criticized her for choosing Burma over her own family.

Her commitment to the cause of freedom was brought to the ultimate test in January 1999, when she learned that Aris was terminally ill with cancer. It had already spread to his lungs and spine, and he likely only had a few months to live. Worse still, he would not be allowed to visit Suu Kyi.

Aung San Suu Kyi's car is stopped on a bridge outside of Rangoon. Suu Kyi spent five days in the car after authorities stopped her from traveling to meet supporters in the country town of Bessein.

A Burmese child holds a poster during a protest rally against the Burmese military junta in front of the Burmese Embassy in Bangkok, Thailand, on October 21, 2007.

KEEPING THE DREAM ALIVE

When she received news of Michael's cancer, it had been more than three years since Suu Kyi last saw him and her children. For a second time, now with her husband's life on the line, she faced the dilemma of whether to leave Burma. If she left the country for any circumstances, she would not be allowed to return. Suu Kyi would have been consigned to lifelong exile, and those close to her in Burma would have been rounded up by the governing junta.

Before her marriage to Aris in 1972, Suu Kyi had repeatedly expressed in letters to him her worry that one day she might have to choose Burma over all else. "Sometimes I am beset by fears," she wrote, "that circumstances and national considerations might tear us apart just when we are so happy in each other that separation would be torment."

Suu Kyi decided to stay in Burma. Michael Aris passed away on March 27, 1999, without seeing his wife of twenty-six years a final time. March 27 was also his birthday.

Four years earlier, in his forward to *Freedom From Fear*, Aris had considered the circumstances of his life. "Fate and history never seem to work in orderly ways," he wrote. "Timings are unpredictable and do not wait upon conveniences."

A year after Michael Aris's death Suu Kyi was put under house arrest for attempting to leave Rangoon for a political meeting. She was released two years later, only to be rearrested and put back under house arrest in 2003.

The 2003 arrest occurred after Suu Kyi returned from a visit to Kachin State. On the evening of May 30, a large gang armed with bamboo staves, iron pipes, and slingshots ambushed her motorcade, near the town of Depayin. (The incident is referred to as the Depayin Massacre because of where it took place.) Suu Kyi escaped unharmed, but up to one hundred of her supporters are believed to have been beaten to death. The military took her into "protective custody," allegedly for her own good, and then put her under house arrest. The attackers were members of a pro-military-regime group known as the Union of Solidarity and Development Association (USDA). Established in the 1990s by Burma's military regime, the USDA was supposed to be a "social organization," created to organize grassroots support for the military. Instead, the USDA became the military junta's jackboot.

INTERNATIONAL SANCTIONS AND PROTESTS

Starting in the 1990s, the United States, Canada, Australia, and the European Union began imposing tough economic sanctions against Burma. The U.S. government prohibited new investment in Burma, either by individuals or entities, and imposed a ban on imports and exports. Top Burmese officials and Burmese financial institutions had their overseas assets frozen, and visa restrictions were placed on members of the military regime and their families and allies.

While many Western nations ceased to trade with Burma, the trade group ASEAN (Association of Southeast Asian Nations) admitted Burma to its ranks in 1997. Indonesia was quick to let it be known it would not criticize any country in this association; investment from China and India increased. According to one report, Burma is "the prom queen that both China and India want to dance with."

A group of protesters hold a silent demonstration outside the meeting place for the ASEAN group in Kuala Lumpur, Malaysia, on July 23, 1997, in solidarity with the people of Burma and other parts of Southeast Asia who continued to be killed, jailed, tortured, and harassed.

China began supporting Burma by offering its neighbor debt relief, economic development grants, and construction loans. In return Burma offered China its hydrocarbon resources, its friendly army of some 400,000 soldiers, and access to any facilities on its coast on the Bay of Bengal. Natural gas accounts for more than half of Burma's exports, and once a pipeline carrying gas from Burma's Shwe and Shuephyu fields to China's Yunnan Province begins to flow, natural gas exports are expected to increase even more. The estimated date of completion of the pipeline is 2014.

Military ties with China and India strengthened as well, with China purportedly supplying Burma with arms and munitions.

By the 1990s, Burma's drug trade had made it the world's dominant heroin producer— that is until priced out of the market by Afghanistan. With the loss in heroin traffic, the drug producers turned instead to methamphetamine, which relies on chemicals coming in from China. To add further to the concerns about Burma, at a security conference in Thailand, Hillary Clinton, the U.S. secretary of state, learned from Burmese defectors of the country receiving assistance from North Korea in "an alleged elaborate program to develop nuclear weapons."

Present-day Burma is not so far removed from the totalitarian police state of Orwell's *1984*. The Burmese army has been fighting armed ethnic groups and insurgents since independence in 1948. As much as 40 percent of the country's budget is spent on the army, while only around 1 percent goes toward the health and education of the Burmese people.

A young ethnic Karen cries, huddling against the rain as he and his family members run from Burmese soldiers near their village in the Toungoo district of eastern Burma.

More than 2,000 political activists, journalists, artists, and workers languish in Burma's squalid prisons. And there are wide restrictions on opposition parties and severe limits on basic freedom of expression, association, and assembly. Burma has a standing law that bans all gatherings of more than five people.

Foreign news agencies and wire services such as the Associated Press, Reuters, and Agence France-Press are not allowed in Burma. They are only allowed to use Burmese stringers; Chinese correspondents are the only foreign press permitted to work there on a full-time basis. Military censors also tightly control and monitor all Internet use. It is illegal to own an unregistered modem in Burma, and foreign news and social networking sites are blocked. As of 2009, only one in 455 Burmese were Internet users, and Internet cafes in the major cities of Rangoon and Mandalay charged around forty cents an hour for access, which is too expensive. The per capita annual income in Burma is $280—less than eighty cents a day.

Tourists and visitors to Burma are monitored as well; the authoritarian regime requires hotels and guesthouses to furnish information about the identities and activities of their foreign guests. Hollywood actress Michelle Yeoh, who is slated to play the part of Suu Kyi in a forthcoming movie, has been barred from entering Burma. Burmese military officials deported the forty-eight-year-old actress, famous for her role in the 1997 James Bond film *Tomorrow Never Dies*, the same day she arrived in Rangoon, on June 22, 2011. No explanation was given, and Yeoh is barred from entering the country, indefinitely.

The trafficking of women, children, and men for forced labor and sexual exploitation is yet another problem associated with Burma. Burma has been identified in the world community as a major source for these illicit activities, and the country remains the world's second-largest producer of opium.

The United Nations has ranked Burma as one of the twenty poorest countries in the world. One in three children is malnourished, malaria is endemic, and thousands of Burmese people have died of AIDS, largely because retroviral drug treatment is hard, if not impossible, to get outside of the major cities. Power outages are a feature of everyday life (80 percent of Burmese live without electricity), cell phones rarely work (only 4 percent of the population are wired to telephone networks, one of the world's lowest telephone usage rates), and travel along unpaved, dirt tracks is the norm, rather than the exception.

THE SAFFRON REVOLUTION

Suu Kyi remained locked up and powerless to counter the sad state of affairs. She could only listen to BBC and Asia Pacific radio reports of what was going on in her native land.

One of the things Suu Kyi would have learned listening to the radio was that Burma's military generals relocated the capital from Rangoon to Naypyitaw, a new town carved out of the countryside. Naypyitaw, which translates to Abode of the Kings, is about three hundred miles north of Rangoon. Why the military rulers moved the capital and how much it cost to relocate there is unclear. But the new capital, built in secret and in a relatively remote location, may have cost between $4 and $5 billion, according to one expert on Burma's economy. Whatever the cost, the capital city stands in stark contrast to the rest of the country. Naypyitaw has smooth ten-lane roads with manicured roundabouts, five golf courses, an Olympic-size soccer stadium, and a large zoo, with an air-conditioned penguin house. Most people who live near the zoo are villagers and cannot afford the price of admission.

In August 2007, the ruling junta unexpectedly raised fuel prices steeply to further impoverish its people, not realizing how much anger this would generate. Yet again, the Buddhist monks broke their vows against participating in political protests by leading a series of rallies. Photos of these tens of thousands of monks dressed in their saffron robes leading tens of thousands of civilians made headline news in every major newspaper in the world. Counting on the age of the Internet, the monks hoped their Saffron Revolution would reach the ears of others outside their country's borders.

Buddhist monks march and pray during a peaceful protest against the military government on the streets of Rangoon in September 2007.

Alarmed at the uprising, the junta regime brutally suppressed the protests, killing at least thirteen people and arresting thousands, including Internet blogger Nay Phone Latt, who was given a twelve-year jail term—a harsh reminder of what happens to those who dare to use the Internet to speak out against the ruling junta. Military rulers allowed Suu Kyi to step out of her house long enough to address the monks with a plea for no violence before insisting once again that she step back inside. Since then, there have been reports that the regime has continued to raid homes and monasteries and arrest people suspected of participating in pro-democracy protests.

In June 2009, Suu Kyi was expected to walk free. However, on May 3, 2009, four weeks before her scheduled release, a fifty-three-year-old American named John Yettaw showed up unexpectedly at her villa. Yettaw, a Mormon father of seven, swam a mile across Inya Lake to reach Suu Kyi. He claimed that God warned him in a vision of Suu Kyi's impending assassination, and he needed to alert her.

John Yettaw
in 2009

It was not the first time that Yettaw had attempted to reach Suu Kyi; it was the third. In November of 2008 he had shown up at the house by walking along an open drain, but Yettaw had failed to meet his heroine.

This third time he made it. Suu Kyi was startled by his sudden arrival. She asked him to leave, but relented when he complained of hunger and exhaustion. "Obviously I didn't want to send him back out into the lake to be drowned," said Suu Kyi. "I felt I could not hand over anybody to be arrested by the authorities when so many of our people who had been arrested had not been given a fair hearing. It was a matter of principle."

Yettaw, a diabetic who used flippers made out of plastic bottles, stayed overnight before turning himself over to the armed guards. As a result of having an unscheduled visitor while under house arrest, Suu Kyi and the two women assistants living with her were charged with violating the terms of her house arrest. So was Yettaw. The four were sent to Insein Prison, in Rangoon.

If found guilty, Suu Kyi would face five years in prison. Yettaw believed that he was helping the cause for freedom in Burma, but others felt he had jeopardized the movement and Suu Kyi. Htay Aung, a former Burmese political prisoner in exile in Thailand, stated that Yettaw's actions made "the complications more complicated. Now we don't know what's going to happen to Burma."

In a carefully staged event, on August 13, 2009, Aung San Suu Kyi reported to a Burmese courtroom for her trial. Now a slight and composed woman in her sixties, she was led into the courtroom to hear the verdict. As the world waited for news, she was informed that she was sentenced to three years of hard labor for allowing an American to stay overnight in her compound without gaining prior approval from the government. After allowing for a few minutes of stunned silence to fill the courtroom, General Than Shwe, the leader of the ruling military junta, rose to grandly read a commutation statement. With an elaborate gesture, he informed the courtroom that Suu Kyi would instead serve an additional eighteen months of house arrest. These charges were

Burmese security guards building a fence at Suu Kyi's
lakeside house prior to the election

carefully designed to keep her under house arrest until after a general election in November 2010. Yettaw was sentenced to seven years in prison, but was released days later to United States senator Jim Webb. Webb became the first member of Congress in ten years to visit Burma.

THE DREAM OF DEMOCRACY

On November 7, 2010, for the first time in twenty years, Burma held elections, staged to put the country one step closer to its "road map" to limited democracy, or as the generals put it, "discipline-flourishing democracy." Because Suu Kyi's party considered Burma's election laws unfair, the National League for Democracy (NLD) did not participate, and according to new election laws, this meant it had to disband. A group of younger NLD members formed a new party called the National Democratic Force; its members argued that some representation in the new parliament was better than none at all. In the end, though, and to no one's surprise, the pro-junta USDA party won in a landslide victory.

Western countries and the United Nations condemned the outcome, saying it was rigged and rampant with fraud. President Barack Obama said Burma's election was neither free nor fair and had not met "any of the internationally accepted standards associated with legitimate elections." India, on the other hand, called the election free and fair, and China made no criticism of Burma.

Five days after the election Daw Aung San Suu Kyi was released from her family's home, where the generals had kept her for fifteen of the past twenty-one years. She was greeted by thousands of jubilant supporters who had gathered outside of her compound. Around the world thousands more celebrated. Then ten days later Suu Kyi was reunited with her younger son, Kim Aris, who had traveled to Thailand before his mother's release and waited to be granted a visa to Burma. Mother and son had not seen each other in a decade.

Suu Kyi walks arm in arm with her son Kim Aris during their visit to Shwedagon Pagoda in Rangoon on November 24, 2010. During her years of house arrest, Suu Kyi spent long hours meditating. She, like most Burmese, practices Theravada Buddhism, which emphasizes individual salvation.

Since her release, "the Lady," as Suu Kyi is widely and affectionately known in Burma, has traveled around her country but only in her capacity as a private citizen. She is not allowed to give public speeches; though, she is often surrounded by pro-democracy supporters.

Suu Kyi has also met several times with officials of the new, nominally civilian government that took control from the military junta in March 2011. The new government has shown signs of openness, by releasing two hundred of Burma's political prisoners, rewriting laws on taxes and property ownership, suspending an unpopular Chinese-funded dam project, and loosening restrictions on the media. These gradual moves toward democracy have prompted Suu Kyi's National League for Democracy to rejoin politics and register for future elections, and The Lady has even announced plans to run for a seat in parliament. Still, basic freedoms and genuine democracy remains a distant reality.

In the summer of 2011, Suu Kyi gave a lecture on "Liberty," which was broadcast on BBC Radio. The lecture was recorded in secret and smuggled out of Burma. Suu Kyi gave a firsthand account of the fight against tyranny in Burma, and she shared her thoughts on "what freedom means to me and to others across the world who are still in the sad state of what I would call unfreedom." Then she closed her lecture by reciting her favorite lines from Rudyard Kipling's *Kim*:

> I'd not give room for an Emperor-
> I'd hold my road for a King.
> To the Triple Crown I'd not bow down-
> But this is a different thing!
> I'll not fight with the Powers of Air-
> Sentry, pass him through!
> Drawbridge let fall—He's the lord of us all—
> The Dreamer whose dream came true!"

For now, Aung San Suu Kyi's dreams for a democratic Burma are unfulfilled. But she remains ever hopeful. "Freedom and democracy," Suu Kyi says, "are dreams you never give up."

Looking straight ahead to the future, Aung San Suu Kyi walks through woods near her home.

Burmese soldiers confront demonstrators during the
1988 crackdown that ignited Suu Kyi's political activism.

TIMELINE

1945 Born on June 19 in Rangoon, Burma, to General Aung San, commander of the Burma Independence Army, and Khin Kyi, a nurse.

1947 Father Aung San, a national hero, is assassinated by rivals in Rangoon on July 19.

1960 Moves to New Delhi, India, with her mother, Burma's ambassador to India.

1964 Enters Oxford University.

1969 Completes her BA in economics, politics, and philosophy at Oxford University.

1969 Moves to New York to work for the United Nations.

1972 Marries British academic Michael Aris and moves with him to Bhutan.

1973 First son, Alexander Aris, is born in London.

1977 Second son, Kim Aris, is born in Oxford.

1985 Research fellowships at Kyoto University in Japan and the Institute of Advanced Studies in Simla, India.

1988 Returns to Burma to be with her ailing mother; makes her first public speech, addressing half a million people at the Shwedagon rally; named general secretary of the newly formed National League for Democracy (NLD).

1989 Placed under house arrest; Burma renamed Myanmar.

1991 Awarded the Nobel Peace Prize.

1995 Released from house arrest.

1999 Husband Michael dies of cancer.

2000 Confined to house arrest a second time after defying travel restrictions.

2002 Released from house arrest.

2003 Placed in Insein Prison and later returned to house arrest.

2007 House arrest extended by one year; appears in public for first time since 2003 to pray with protesting Buddhist monks.

2009 Sentenced to an additional eighteen months of house arrest after an American civilian swam the lake bordering her home and spent the night at her compound.

2010 Greeted by thousands of jubilant supporters after her detention order expires on November 13.

Sources

Chapter One: BURMA, "LAND OF CHARM AND CRUELTY"

p. 11,   "terribly frightened . . ." Whitney Stewart, *Aung San Suu Kyi: Fearless Voice of Burma* (Minneapolis: Lerner Publications Company, 1997), 32.

p. 11,   "the first few days . . ." Ibid.

p. 11,   "I wandered around . . ." John Pilger, "My Last Conversation With Aung San Suu Kyi," *New Statesman*, October 8, 2007, 22.

p. 11,   "The only real prison . . ." Alan Clements, *Instinct for Freedom: Finding Liberation Through Living* (California: New World Library, 2002), 244.

p. 12,   "vividly cosmopolitan [city that] outshone . . ." Justin Wintle, *Perfect Hostage: A Life of Aung San Suu Kyi, Burma's Prisoner of Conscience* (New York: Skyhorse Publishing, 2007), 44.

p. 16,   "The peasants rose . . ." Ibid., 58-59.

p. 19,   "golden land," Alan Clements and Leslie Kean, *Burma's Revolution of the Spirit: The Struggle for Democratic Freedom and Dignity* (Bangkok: White Orchid Press, 1995), 11.

p. 19,   "the pearl of Asia," Ibid.

p. 19,   "East is East . . ." Rudyard Kipling, "The Ballad of East and West," Bartleby.com/246/1129.html.

p. 19,   "quite unlike any land . . ." Rudyard Kipling, *Works of Rudyard Kipling. From Sea to Sea: Letters of Travel. American Notes* (New York: Doubleday, Page & Company, 1915), 203.

p. 19,   "land of charm and cruelty," Peter Carey, review of *Perfect Hostage: A Life of Aung San Suu Kyi*, by Justin Wintle, *Oxford Today* 19, no. 3 (Trinity Issue 2007): 49.

p. 20,   "Burma is one of those . . ." Aung San Suu Kyi, *Freedom From Fear* (New York: Penguin Books, 1991), 39.

p. 21,   "Where the flyin' fishes play . . ." Rudyard Kipling, "Mandalay," Poetry Lovers' Page, www.poetryloverspage.com/poets/kipling/mandalay.html.

p. 21,   "If you want a picture . . ." George Orwell, *Nineteen Eighty-Four* (Fairfield, IA: 1st World Library-Literary Society, 2004), 334.

Chapter Two: The Assassination of Aung San

p. 26,   "double life, nurturing . . ." Wintle, *Perfect Hostage*, 115.

p. 27,   "Our army will fight for the benefit of the country . . ." Ibid., 121.

p. 34,   "admiration for Aung San . . ." Ibid., 150.

p. 35,   "Everyone referred to my father as Bogyoke . . ." Ibid., 155.

p. 35,   "One can't die . . ." "Myanmar's Famous Proverbs: Lawka Niti Rules," http://www.myanmars.net/myanmar-language/myanmar-proverbs.htm.

Chapter Three: Leaving Burma for India

p. 38,   "[My great aunt] was always telling stories . . ." Stewart, *Fearless Voice of Burma*, 26.

p. 38,   "How could Bugs Bunny's . . ." Wintle, *Perfect Hostage*, 155.

p. 38,   "The first autobiography . . ." Aung San Suu Kyi, "Liberty," Reith Lectures 2011, BBC Radio 4, June 28, 2011, radio broadcast, www.bbc.co.uk/programmes/b0126d29.

p. 39,   "I think in some way . . ." Stewart, *Fearless Voice of Burma*, 30.

p. 40,   "From my earliest childhood . . ." John Parenteau, *Prisoner for Peace: Aung San Suu Kyi and Burma's Struggle for Democracy* (Greensboro, NC: Morgan Reynolds, 1994), 61.

Chapter Four: Oxford, London, Love & New York

p.45,   "the daughter of some or other . . ." Wintle, *Perfect Hostage*, 174.

p. 46,   "inherited social grace . . ." Ann Pasternak Slater, "Suu Burmese," in Aung San Suu Kyi, *Freedom from Fear* (New York: Viking, 1991), 258.

pp. 46-47, "At the very end . . ." Ibid., 261.

p. 47,   "Suu had the knack . . ." Wintle, *Perfect Hostage*, 176.

p. 47,   "unusual purity of mind . . ." Ibid., 177.

p. 47,   "Suu Burmese," Pasternak Slater, "Suu Burmese," in Aung San Suu Kyi, *Freedom from Fear,* 259.

p. 47,   "She was curious to experience . . ." Parenteau, *Prisoner for Peace*, 67.

p. 49,   "almost everything I know about economics . . ." Wintle, *Perfect Hostage*, 179.

p. 49,   "My lasting impression of her . . ." Ibid., 178.

p. 49,   "Is there something funny? . . ." Ibid., 178-179.

p. 55,   "Staff members of the UN . . ." Ma Than É, "A Flowering of the Spirit: Memories of Suu and Her Family," in Aung San Suu Kyi, *Freedom from Fear*, 250-251.

p. 56,   "always seemed to take . . ." Wintle, *Perfect Hostage*, 203.

p. 57,   "We decided that we should have a rehearsal . . ." Wintle, *Pefect Hostage*, 203.

p. 57,   "there was more to this invitation . . ." Ma Than É, "A Flowering of the Spirit: Memories of Suu and Her Family," in Aung San Suu Kyi, *Freedom from Fear*, 251.

p. 59,   "being the daughter of . . ." Wintle, *Perfect Hostage*, 205.

Chapter Five: MARRIAGE AND MOTHERHOOD

p. 62,   "I only ask one thing . . ." Michael Aris, "Introduction," in Aung San Suu Kyi, *Freedom from Fear*, xvii.

p. 63,   "a tiny and remote kingdom . . ." Wintle, *Perfect Hostage*, 206.

p. 66,   "welcome and uncomplainingly entertain . . ." Philip Kreager, "Aung San Suu Kyi and the Peaceful Struggle for Human Rights in Burma," in Aung San Suu Kyi, *Freedom from Fear*, 298.

p. 67,   "required a wind-dried . . ." Wintle, *Perfect Hostage*, 213.

p. 72,   "were able to use the English language . . ." Aung San Suu Kyi, "Intellectual Life in Burma and India under Colonialism," in Aung San Suu Kyi, *Freedom from Fear*, 105.

p. 73,   "dissatisfied with a life . . ." Pasternak Slater, "Suu Burmese," in Aung San Suu Kyi, *Freedom from Fear*, 264-265.

p. 73,   "one of the few . . ." Ibid., 265.

p. 73,   "It was a quiet evening in Oxford . . ." Aris, "Introduction," in Aung San Suu Kyi, *Freedom from Fear*, xv.

Chapter Six: RETURNING TO BURMA

p. 82,   "What horrifies me every . . ." Wintle, *Perfect Hostage*, 245.

p. 85,   "Suu's house quickly became the main . . ." Aris,
            "Introduction," in Aung San Suu Kyi, *Freedom from Fear*,
            xviii.

p. 85,   "a second mother . . ." Wintle, *Perfect Hostage*, 308.

p. 86,   "As I consider that . . ." Ibid., 254.

p. 87,   "Butcher of Rangoon," Ibid., 255.

p. 91,   "The people's nurses . . ." Ibid., 263.

p. 93,   "It is the students . . ." Parenteau, *Prisoner of Peace*, 100.

p. 93,   "It is true that I have lived . . ." Aung San Suu Kyi, "Speech
            to a Mass Rally at the Shwedagon Pagoda," in Aung San
            Suu Kyi, *Freedom from Fear*, 199.

p. 93,   "Some people have been saying . . ." Ibid.

pp. 93-94, "Since my father . . ." Ibid.

p. 94,   "We must make democracy the popular creed . . ." Ibid.,
            200.

p. 95,   "What surprised me . . ." Wintle, *Perfect Hostage*, 264.

Chapter Seven: THE DEMOCRACY MOVEMENT TAKES SHAPE

p. 97,   "be of most use in bringing about . . ." Aung San Suu Kyi,
            "The Objectives," in Aung San Suu Kyi, *Freedom from Fear*,
            207.

p. 97,   "democratic credentials were second . . . " Parenteau,
            Prisoner for Peace, 105.

p. 100,   "Why do you think . . ." Ibid., 107.

p. 100,   "devastating civil war . . ." Wintle, *Perfect Hostage*, 267.

p. 102,   "a free-for-all election campaign . . ." Ibid., 287.

p. 102,   "indiscriminate killing . . ." Aung San Suu Kyi, "Letter to
            the Ambassadors," in Aung San Suu Kyi, *Freedom from
            Fear*, 217.

p. 109,   "For twenty-two days . . ." Wintle, *Perfect Hostage*, 330.

p. 109,   "very obviously the [SLORC's] plan . . ." Aris,
            "Introduction," in Aung San Suu Kyi, *Freedom from Fear*,
            xxiii.

p. 112,   "the days I spent alone with her . . ." Wintle, *Perfect
            Hostage*, 333.

p. 112,   "the authorities had hoped . . ." Aris, "Introduction," in Aung San Suu Kyi, *Freedom from Fear*, xxiii.

Chapter Eight: POLITICAL PRISONER AND
                NOBEL LAUREATE

p. 115,   "to avoid a feckless . . ." Aung San Suu Kyi, "Letter from Burma (No. 15): Days of Rest Life," *Mainichi Daily News*, March 4, 1996, www.burmalibrary.org/docs/Letters_from_ Burma.htm.

p. 116,   "In Burma, one should . . ." Ibid., "Letter from Burma (No. 32): A Dissident's Life."

p. 116,   "I think of him . . ." Barbara Bradley, "No Signs of Freedom in Burma's Nobel House," *Insight on the News*, July 25, 1994.

p. 118,   "torture, including electric shocks . . ." Parenteau, *Prisoner for Peace*, 123.

p. 120,   "malnutrition, lack of access to safe water . . ." Aung San Suu Kyi, *Letters from Burma* (London: Penguin Books, 1997), 57.

p. 120,   "bring[ing] out something of the best in us . . ." Wintle, *Perfect Hostage*, 352.

p. 120,   "I know that she would begin by saying . . ." Ibid.

p. 121,   "Many will now for the first time . . ." Aris, "Introduction," in Aung San Suu Kyi, *Freedom from Fear*, xxvii-xxviii.

p. 122,   "We, her family, are denied any contact . . ." Ibid., xxviii.

p. 123,   "A political prisoner failed . . ." Suu Kyi, *Letters from Burma*, 24.

p. 126,   "Nothing has changed since . . ." Alan Clements, "We Are Still Prisoners in Our Own Country: An Interview with Aung San Suu Kyi," *Humanist*, November-December 1997.

p. 126,   "The human rights situation . . ." Bradley, "No Signs of Freedom in Burma's Nobel House."

pp. 126-127, "Khin Nyunt [head of military intelligence] expressed the belief . . ." Wintle, *Perfect Hostage*, 370.

p. 127,   "no, and I think . . ." Clements, "We Are Still Prisoners in Our Own Country: An Interview with Aung San Suu Kyi."

p. 127,   "I made the decision . . ." Leslie Kean and Dennis Bernstein, "Aung San Suu Kyi Interview," *Progressive*, March 1997.

p. 131,   "Sometimes I am beset . . ." Aris, "Introduction," in Aung San Suu Kyi, *Freedom from Fear*, xvii.

p. 131,   "Fate and history . . ." Ibid., xviii.

p. 132,   "the prom queen . . ." International Crisis Group, "China's Myanmar Dilemma," *Asia Report* 117 (2009), 28.

p. 134,   "an alleged elaborate . . ." "More Bricks in the Wall Around Her: The Junta Cocks Another Snook at the Burmese People and Foreign Opinion," *Economist*, August 13, 2009.

p. 139,   "Obviously I didn't want . . ." Joshua Hammer, "A Free Woman," *New Yorker*, January 24, 2011.

p. 139,   "the complications more complicated . . ." Tony Dokoupil, F. De Burgo-Naughton and Lennox Samuels, "The Lady and the Tramp," *Newsweek*, June 22, 2009.

p. 142,   "discipline-flourishing democracy," Rachel Harvey, "Burma: Hopes and Fears Over New Political System," BBC News (Asia Pacific), March 30, 2011, http://www.bbc.co.uk/ news/world-asia-pacific-12896815.

p.142,   "any of the internationally . . ." "Burma (Myanmar) Country Specific Information," U.S. State Department, http://travel.state.gov/travel/cis_pa_tw/cis/cis_1077.html.

p. 144,   "what freedom means . . ." Suu Kyi, "Liberty," Reith Lectures 2011, BBC Radio 4.

p. 144,   "Freedom and democracy . . ." "Aung San Suu Kyi Interview: Myanmar Democracy Advocate Gives First U.S. Television Interview," *Huffington Post World*, January 21, 2011, www.huffingtonpost.com/2011/01/21/aung-san-suu-kyi-interview_n_812486.html.

Back Cover

"We haven't seen . . ." Seth Mydans and Liz Robbens, "Myanmar Junta Frees Dissident; Crowds Gather," *New York Times*, November 14, 2010.

Bibliography

Altman, Alex, Harriet Barovick, Alyssa Fetini, Laura Fitzpatrick, Randy James, Frances Romero, M. J. Stephey, and Claire Suddath. "10 Essential Stories." *Time*, August 24, 2009.

Bono. "Aung San Suu Kyi: Unbearable Choices." *Time*, April 26, 2004.

Bradley, Barbara. "No Signs of Freedom in Burma's Nobel House." *Insight on the News*, July 25, 1994.

Clements, Alan. "We Are Still Prisoners in Our Own Country: An Interview with Aung San Suu Kyi." *Humanist*, November-December 1997.

Clifton, Tony. "She Is Not Alone." *Newsweek*, July 24, 1995.

Dokoupil, Tony, F. De Burgo-Naughton, and Lennox Samuels. "The Lady and the Tramp." *Newsweek*, June 22, 2009.

Economist. "Myanmar's Hidden Threats." November 2, 1991.

———. "Talking at Last to Aung San Suu Kyi; Talks in Myanmar?" January 13, 2001.

———. "No Road to Mandalay." September 30, 2000.

———. "Glass Rods and Steel Wires." July 22, 1995.

———. "Regime Unchanged; Myanmar and ASEAN." October 11, 2003.

———. "Shame in Myanmar." April 3, 1999.

———. "Asia's Mandela?" July 15, 1995.

———. "A New Game in Myanmar." June 1, 1996.

———. "More Bricks in the Wall Around Her: The Junta Cocks Another Snook at the Burmese People and Foreign Opinion," August 13, 2009.

———. "Who Speaks for the People?" January 27, 1996.

———. "The Saffron Revolution." September 29, 2007.

Fuller, Thomas. "Myanmar High Court to Consider Dissident's Appeal." *New York Times*, December 4, 2009.

Gajewski, Karen Ann. "Amnesty International Has Named Aung San Suu Kyi the Recipient of Its Prestigious Ambassador of Conscience Award." *Humanist*, September-October 2009.

Kean, Leslie, and Dennis Bernstein. "Aung San Suu Kyi Interview." *Progressive*, March 1997.

Kyi, Aung San Suu. "Light at the End of the Struggle (Portrait of Strength)." *O, The Oprah Magazine*, April 2002.

———. *Freedom from Fear.* London: Penguin Books, 1991.

———. *Letters from Burma.* London: Penguin Books, 1997.

———. *The Voice of Hope.* Conversations with Alan Clements. New York: Seven Stories Press, 2008.

Mcdonald, Mark. "Myanmar Dissident's Trial Resumes." *New York Times*, July 11, 2009.

Mydans, Seth. "Burmese Activist Receives New Term of House Arrest." *New York Times*, August 12, 2009.

———. "Burmese Officials Deny Dissident Was Injured." *New York Times*, June 4, 2003.

———. "Burmese Daily at Odds With Democracy Advocate." *New York Times*, January 19, 2007.

———. "A Year After Vowing Change, Burmese Junta Hardens Line." *New York Times*, May 30, 2003.

———. "Burmese Opposition Supports New U.S. Approach." *New York Times*, September 24, 2009.

———. "A Burmese Icon Tends a Flickering Flame." *New York Times*, July 12, 2009.

New York Times. "Ending Repression in Myanmar." May 7, 2002.

Parenteau, John. *Prisoner for Peace: Aung San Suu Kyi and Burma's Struggle for Democracy.* Greensboro, NC: Morgan Reynolds Publishing, 1994.

Pilger, John. "With an Eye to its Vast Asian Market, Europe Promotes Human Rights When the Price Is Right." *New Statesman*, January 24, 2005.

Sardar, Ziauddin. "Kept in Power by Male Fantasy." *New Statesman*, August 7, 1998.

Stewart, Whitney. *Aung San Suu Kyi: Fearless Voice of Burma.* Minneapolis: Lerner Publications Company, 1997.

Thant Myint-U. *The Rivers of Lost Footsteps: Histories of Burma.* New York: Farrar, Straus and Giroux, 2006.

Wintle, Justin. *Perfect Hostage: A Life of Aung San Suu Kyi, Burma's Prisoner of Conscience.* New York: Skyhorse Publishing, 2007.

WEB SITES

http://www.nobel.se/peace/laureates/1991/kyi-bio.html

Summary of the major events and accomplishments of
Aung San Suu Kyi.

**http://www.lib.berkeley.edu/SSEAL/SouthAsia/sahist_burma.
html**

This UC Berkeley site contains links to an extensive online Burma
library, which lists thousands of articles and scholarship related to
Burma, including the country's pre-history; its time under British
rule; the profiles, speeches, writings, and interviews of historically
important figures such as Aung San Suu Kyi; and videos and photo-
graphs of Suu Kyi.

http://www.bbc.co.uk/programmes/b0126d29

Click on this link to listen to Aung San Suu Kyi deliver lectures on
"Liberty" and "Dissent" during the BBC's 2011 Reith Lectures.

http://www.ibiblio.org/obl/docs/Letters_from_Burma.htm

This link takes you to the fifty-two "Letters from Burma" written
by Aung San Suu Kyi between November 27, 1995, and December
9, 1996. The series was originally published in the Monday morning
editions of the *Mainichi Shimban* and the *Mainichi Daily News*, and later
turned into a book.

INDEX

PHOTO CREDITS

All images used in this book that are not in the public domain are credited in the listing that follows: